The Making of
Stan Laurel

The Making of Stan Laurel

Echoes of a British Boyhood

DANNY LAWRENCE

McFarland & Company, Inc., Publishers

Jefferson, North Carolina, and London

LIBRARY OF CONGRESS CATALOGUING-IN-PUBLICATION DATA

Lawrence, Danny, 1940–
    The making of Stan Laurel : echoes of a British boyhood /
Danny Lawrence.
        p.   cm.
    Includes bibliographical references and index.

    ISBN 978-0-7864-6312-1
    softcover : 50# alkaline paper ∞

    1. Laurel, Stan — Childhood and youth.   2. Motion picture
actors and actresses — United States — Biography.   3. Comedians —
Great Britain — Biography.   I. Title
PN2287.L285L39   2011
791.4302'8092 — dc22   [B]   2011013993

BRITISH LIBRARY CATALOGUING DATA ARE AVAILABLE

Front cover: Stan Laurel (Photofest); painting by George D. Thomson of
the High Light in evening sunlight near Stan Laurel's boyhood home in
North Shields.

Manufactured in the United States of America

*McFarland & Company, Inc., Publishers
    Box 611, Jefferson, North Carolina 28640
    www.mcfarlandpub.com*

To my family,
who mean so much to me:
Helen
John and David
Claire and Alison
Jack and Katy, Anna and Finn

Table of Contents

Preface

What makes this book distinctive is its focus on the relationship between Stan Laurel the man and Stan Laurel the boy. Stan Laurel the man was the internationally acclaimed comic genius who lived in the United States. Stan Laurel the boy was the unknown Arthur Stanley Jefferson who grew up in the little-known town of North Shields at the entrance to the River Tyne in northeast England. Stan's theatrical family background and his formative boyhood years gave him an intimate introduction to the world of entertainment and a passionate ambition to spend the rest of his life making people laugh. *The Making of Stan Laurel* examines his family background, his boyhood years and the way in which they affected his future career. Stan, of course, was much more than a supreme comic actor. He was the primary creative force behind the Laurel and Hardy partnership; this book also shows how his boyhood experiences are echoed in the themes found in many of their films.

Stan the man never forgot his life as Stan the boy. Friendships forged in his boyhood years lasted a lifetime and he corresponded and reminisced with people from the northeast of England until his death at age 74 in 1965. Just as Stan remembered his boyhood home, so the world has remembered Stan Laurel, despite the fact that he made his last film in the middle of the last century. Just as he continued to take an interest in his boyhood town, even when living 5,000 miles away, so the world has continued to take an interest in his life and his work, even after so many other Hollywood stars of his era have been all but forgotten. Laurel and Hardy's films are still sold, watched and, above all, enjoyed by hundreds of thousands of people throughout the world. They were churned out at an astonishing rate, and may lack the finesse of today's technically more sophisticated productions, but they have timeless and universal qualities which are still valued and appreciated. The fact that they were shot on monochrome film stock with less than hi-fi soundtracks is inconsequential.

Those who enjoy Laurel and Hardy films will find new material as well as food for thought in this book. It will also appeal to anyone interested in how films were made in those far-off days when the cinema was young and the old silent stars had to confront the demands made by the advent of "talkies." Anyone who has watched MGM's *Singin' in the Rain* or seen Andrew Lloyd Webber's *Sunset Boulevard* will know that the coming of sound ended the careers of numerous silent stars. Laurel and Hardy took the transition in their stride and also made foreign versions of their sound films in an innovative way, winning them an even more devoted following in countries where Spanish, Italian, French and German were spoken.

The Making of Stan Laurel will also interest those who, like me, were born or brought up in, or have become exiled from, their ancestral home in the northeast of England. We all learned as children that the great Stan Laurel lived there at some time but that was virtually the full extent of our knowledge. It gives me great pleasure to be able to pass on so much more information about the nature of his relationship with the area than was available to me when I was growing up.

My interest in him dates back to my own boyhood when I learned that the same man who graced the silver screen and made us all laugh had once lived in my own home town of North Shields. Later, I came to realize that my grandfather was a contemporary of Stan Laurel, that my father was born just before Laurel left the area and that my mother came into the world just as Stan was starting his career on the stage. I was born in North Shields in the closing days of 1940, when Stan Laurel at 50 was at the height of his international fame. I was brought up just a short distance from his boyhood home and across from the Town Hall where he was lauded on a return visit in 1947. In 1953, I even appeared on the same spot on the same stage where Stan Laurel had stood during a charity concert the year before. But it was not until I retired from my academic post (as a sociologist at the University of Nottingham) that I was able to set aside enough time to undertake the research necessary to write this book.

My first acknowledgment must be to the enduring creations of Stanley Arthur Jefferson and his partner Oliver Norvell Hardy. Shortly before completing *The Making of Stan Laurel*, I introduced my own grandchildren to their films. Although brought up in a world of PCs, games consoles and high-definition widescreen TVs, they laughed helplessly and asked for more. That is a remarkable achievement for two comic actors born in 1890 and 1892, respectively.

My second acknowledgment must be to A.J. Marriot. It was after reading his impressive and definitive *Laurel and Hardy: The British Tours* that the idea for this book emerged. During a subsequent telephone conversation with him, he urged me, in his own inimitable way, to stop talking about the project and get on with it. Had he been less forthright in his exhortation, I might still have been at the planning stage. Thank you, A.J., for your timely push, valuable advice and permission to quote from your excellent book (http://laurelandhardythebritishtours.com). All those interested in Laurel and Hardy owe you a debt not only for your dedicated research but also your infectious enthusiasm.

Another enthusiast to whom we owe a debt of gratitude is Bernie Hogya, the founder and archivist of the ambitious Stan Laurel Correspondence Archive project (www.lettersfromstan.com). His site, as he puts it so eloquently, "is a totally genuine labor of love. It is a gift to Stan, for years of laughter and incomparable joy! Each and every letter is an important part of the searchable content of the Archive and will forever be made available FOR FREE to fans and researchers alike. There will never be a charge to use the Archive, nor will it ever make a penny in profit from its contents." Thank you, Bernie, for your hard work and generosity.

The staff members at the North Tyneside Local Studies Library at North Shields deserve recognition for the work they have done in collecting, organizing and preserving a wide range of materials on North Shields and the surrounding area. My thanks are due to Eric Hollerton, Alan Hildrew and, more recently, Diane Leggett, Joyce Marti and Kevin Dresser.

I must thank several people for their help with the photographic images used in the book. The inclusion of three personal family photos has been made possible by the generosity of Lois Laurel Hawes (Stan's daughter), Nancy Wardell (Stan's cousin) and Huntley Jefferson Woods (Stan's nephew). Roland Craig, the grandson of Stan's lifelong friend, the photographer Roland Park, has also been kind enough to give me permission to use a photo of Laurel taken on a return visit to his boyhood home.

Copyright issues prevented the use of other Laurel and Hardy images I planned to include. Help with local photos was provided by the North Tyneside Central Library and Stan Bewick, the archivist of the Tynemouth Photographic Society. Bob Olley, the creator of the wonderful Stan Laurel statues that stand in North Shields and Bishop Auckland, has done more than permit me to use his photographs. He has also been generous enough to allow me to rewrite his own descriptions of the eventful journeys they made to their final destinations (see http://www.robertolley.co.uk). Bob is not the only artist I have to thank. George Thomson kindly agreed to let me use his North Shields High Light painting for the cover. I must also record my thanks to *Downtowngal*, who has made her photograph of the Los Angeles stairs used in the making of the Laurel and Hardy film *The Music Box* freely available to all (http://en.wikipedia.org/wiki/The_Music_ Box).

It is not only photographers and artists that I have to thank. Andrew Gough, the family historian, whose meticulous research into his family tree uncovered previously unknown facts about the Jefferson family history which I have been able to draw on and develop, has also been kind enough to allow me to include information from his website: http://freepages. genealogy.rootsweb.ancestry.com/~andrewgough/ACFGough.htm

One person to whom I owe a debt but who is no longer with us to thank, is Robert King of North Shields. His work on the town's theaters proved very valuable. Without it, my understanding of Stan's father's role in the theatrical world of North Shields would have been much more superficial. I must also thank the many earlier authors on Stan Laurel on whose work I have drawn. I may have sometimes reached different conclusions but, even in such instances, I have always derived much of value from these earlier works. Jack Shotton's then unpublished manuscript of his continuing work on aspects of the history of North Shields also proved useful to me when writing a key section of Chapter 7. The singer-songwriter Texas Pete Shovlin must also be thanked for his permission to let me include the lyrics of his touching tribute to Stan Laurel, in his song, *Letter from Stan*. It can be heard on myspace: (http://www.myspace.com/texaspeteshovlin).

Two old friends and former colleagues at the University of Nottingham must also receive my thanks. Professor Brian Lee made many valuable comments on an early draft of the book and Eric Rowe drew my attention to the provisions of the 1884 *Representation of the People Act* which helped resolve an apparent discrepancy in some of the dates I had uncovered.

At a more personal level, I must thank Stan's daughter, Lois Laurel Hawes, his cousin Nancy Wardell and nephew Huntley Jefferson Woods. Talking to them has made me feel just that little bit closer to Stan himself. I hope they feel that this book does him justice. Like Stan, I left North Shields when I was young and, like him, my deep attachment to my boyhood home has never left me. It has been reinforced by my continuing links with relatives who still live in and around North Shields and the many friends I made all those years ago. Amongst them all, I must single out two for special mention. The first is my dear sister Margaret. When we are together, it is never long before we begin to talk — and argue — about the old days. The fact that she is a few years older means that over the years I have learned a great deal from her. The same is true of my friend George Thomson. We may no longer be young enough to walk the streets until the early hours putting the world to rights but the benefit of the passing years is that I have had ample opportunity to glean much from him too about the town that was our boyhood home.

Finally, I must thank my wife Helen. I owe her so much. She encouraged me when my confidence in the project wavered. She has been unstintingly generous in handling the household chores and crises while I have been insulated from them in my study. She has read many drafts of the book and made innumerable valuable suggestions. For all that — and her love — I thank her. Now that the book has been published, I publicly acknowledge that I have run out of excuses and promise that I will at last buckle down and tidy the garage.

When it comes to quoting from Stan Laurel's own correspondence, or quoting from sources originally published in the English version of English, they have been transcribed exactly. In the case of Stan's words, two further notes are needed. The first is that his words contain not only obvious typographical errors but examples of his own idiosyncratic version of English punctuation. The second is that what to many American readers may appear to be spelling mistakes are no more than an emphatic indication that Stan still *favoured* the English spelling of words even after living for so many years in the United States. The spelling and punctuation in the body of the text is U.S. English.

Introduction

Stan Laurel was the creative force behind the most successful double act in the history of cinema comedy. Inevitably, he is remembered most for the fumbling, innocent, boyish persona he adopted on screen. But, off-screen, he was utterly focused in pursuit of his lifelong vocation to make people laugh. Colleagues on- and off-camera readily acknowledged that it was his unconventional conception of how to make comedy films that made the Laurel and Hardy partnership so successful. As a writer and director, as well as an actor, Laurel remains an iconic figure, still lauded for his creative contribution to cinema comedy.

Laurel and Hardy's last film was released in the early 1950s. Yet more than half a century later, our collective memory of them still conjures up such comic images of a well-meaning but inadequate couple creating chaos all around them, that likening contemporary public figures to them has a resonance that requires little or no explanation. Numerous instances could be cited but perhaps the most striking recent example is that of a poster in which the faces of Prime Minister Tony Blair and President George Bush were superimposed on a photograph of Laurel and Hardy following their decision to invade Iraq. Fair or otherwise, the image speaks volumes to those familiar with the nature of Laurel and Hardy's relationship and the typical scenarios in which they appeared on film.

Stan Laurel and his partner Oliver Hardy delighted international film audiences from the 1920s to the '50s and then went on to win a new following amongst younger people when their films were shown on TV and became available for viewing at home in later decades. Unfortunately, the people who commission TV programs today seem to assume that the young can be entertained only with shows that are brash, colorful, loud and ultimately patronizing. So those wonderful old films of Laurel and Hardy, despite their inherent merit and the fact that they are so admired by almost all of today's current comedy stars, are no longer seen on our TV screens. Today's young people are growing up without easy access to the innocent good humor of Laurel and Hardy which earlier generations so much enjoyed.

Even without the help of TV, Laurel and Hardy remain hugely popular and Stan Laurel in particular continues to be lauded for his creative contribution to cinema comedy. "Sons of the Desert" appreciation societies, named after one of Laurel and Hardy's most popular films, are spread throughout the world, and numerous websites are devoted to Laurel and Hardy's life and work. Their films were so popular that they spawned merchandising products which, along with other memorabilia, continue to sell for substantial sums. Their films have recently been re-released on DVD; several plays have been written on aspects of their lives, and public tributes have been paid to them in the tangible form of statues and acknowledgments of the way in which they have influenced many of today's comedy actors.

Stan's talented partner, Oliver Norvell Hardy, was born in America. Many people assume that this was also true of Stan Laurel. The truth is that he was born in England and remained a UK citizen for the whole of his life. Stan Laurel was born Arthur Stanley Jefferson in Ulverston, a small town in the northwest of England. At an early age he moved to Bishop Auckland for a short time and then to North Shields where his father had taken over the lease of the Theatre Royal. Situated at the entrance to the River Tyne in northeast England, North Shields was then a flourishing town. Stan's family moved there when he was about five years old and he stayed until he was 15, when they moved to Glasgow, Scotland. Stan's family home may have been in North Shields for only about 14 percent of his life but they proved to be formative years. His early boyhood experiences fashioned his ambitions and the direction of the rest of his life. They also influenced many of the comedy situations he later created on screen. The relationships he established as a boy, and the affection he continued to feel towards North Shields, meant that he was still actively corresponding with people from the town when he died in 1965 at age 74.

Those familiar with North Shields today may find it difficult to recognize the town of a century ago described in the early chapters of this book. It was then something of a riverside boom town. When Stan lived there, it was flourishing and vibrant: very much in its heyday. The memories of it which Stan took with him to Hollywood were of a lively, expanding place, able to offer its citizens almost anything that they could want. Ironically, North Shields ultimately became a victim of its own success. The development of the local economy first stimulated growth, but then began to bring about the town's decline as a residential, retail and social center. The very industries that made their owners wealthy created environmental conditions they did not find congenial. They began to drift away into the then still relatively unspoiled countryside beyond the wealth-creating part of the town. The Jeffersons joined in that exodus. Still later, the middle classes more generally began to move into the newly built private suburbs in search of a lifestyle that befitted their relative economic success. Finally, as the worst of the housing was cleared from the streets and riverside banks of North Shields from the 1930s, large sections of the working class were moved by the Borough Council away from what Stan called "the old town." Thanks to the advent of cars, buses and the electrified rail network now known as the Metro, the mobile residents of North Shields' suburbs can now shop wherever they want. That has contributed to the downward spiral of the old town of North Shields. With each successive decade, its battle to survive in the face of competition from its much bigger neighbor Newcastle and out-of-town shopping centers becomes tougher.

This pattern of rise and fall in the fortunes of North Shields does not correspond closely with the fortunes of Stan Laurel. When he was at the height of his fame, his beloved "old town" was struggling with the depression of the 1930s. However, by the time that Stan's film career was over and he returned to the town for the final time in 1952, the writing was on the wall for both Stan and North Shields. As Stan's health was deteriorating, so too were his boyhood town's economic fortunes and its corporate pride. There were other changes that were to alter the face of the town. TV was ousting the cinema as the public's main form of entertainment. By the time Stan died, the cinemas in which his films had brought laughter to audiences for decades were closing one by one until not a single cinema was left in North Shields. Just a few years after his death, Saville Street, the town's main shopping thoroughfare, along which he must have walked many hundreds of times between his father's Theatre Royal and his family home, was ripped apart to make way for the entrance to the car park of a never very successful shopping mall. Less than ten years after his death, the County Borough of Tynemouth, of which North Shields was the major part, and in which his father had once been an elected councilor, was no longer even a distinct local authority. With the 1974 reorganization of local government in the UK, it became part of the disparate Borough of North Tyneside.

Some of the townspeople of Ulverston have capitalized on the fact that Stan was born there. A bar and restaurant are named after him and it has a Laurel and Hardy museum which recently re-located into larger premises in, appropriately, a disused cinema. Some years ago the local newspaper published a book, *Laurel Before Hardy*, which focused on the first five years of his life. In 2009, a huge crowd of local people and Laurel and Hardy aficionados turned out for the unveiling of a statue of the famous pair in the town's refurbished County Square outside the Coronation Hall Theatre. It was unveiled by Ken Dodd, probably Britain's most loved comedian. The townspeople of Harlem, where Oliver Hardy was born, also celebrate and capitalize on their association with their famous son. Since 1988 they have hosted an annual Oliver Hardy Festival which draws enormous crowds. In contrast, whilst Stan's association with his boyhood town of North Shields may not be forgotten, it is not celebrated and nothing much has been done to date to capitalize on the link. Moreover, whereas the house where he was born in Ulverston is still standing, both the houses in which he lived in North Shields have been demolished. The only two tangible reminders of the link are a plaque on a house, standing more or less on the site of his first North Shields home (unveiled by his nephew Huntley Jefferson Woods) and Bob Olley's statue of Stan Laurel erected in the center of the square (unveiled not by a relative or national celebrity but by the local Member of Parliament).

North Shields' neglect of Laurel is matched by the neglect of North Shields in Stan Laurel's biographies. With the exception of Marriot's work, what has been written about his association with the town has been superficial. Yet any book that purports to explore the origins of Stan's passion for comedy and his life in the theater and cinema must include the legacy of those boyhood years. *The Making of Stan Laurel* is an attempt to remedy this major omission in the literature. It also includes a significant contribution to the ongoing discussion about the sources of the comedy situations and gags Stan helped to create on screen. It argues that many of them contain echoes of Stan's early life in North Shields. The creative process, whether in comedy or any other artistic field, is not something that permits a simple analysis. However, it is a process into which we can sometimes see telling and tantalizing glimpses. And, from time to time in Stan Laurel's creative work, there are undoubted echoes of North Shields: the town in which he lived for only ten formative years but which stayed close to his heart for the whole of the rest of his life.

Instead of ignoring the significance of his boyhood years, as most other writers have done, this book describes the circumstances which led Stan's father to bring his family to live in North Shields. It records what is known about his family, education and boyhood as well as his father's theatrical empire. It describes the kind of local theatrical world in which the young Stan was brought up at the very start of commercial cinema in the early years of the twentieth century. Previous references to these issues have been mainly superficial. In discussing them, I have had the advantage of being able to draw on local knowledge and sources that may not have been available to earlier writers.

In later chapters I describe the marked fluctuations in Stan Jefferson's career after he left North Shields and struggled to make a living first in variety theaters in the UK and then vaudeville in America. Unlike Charles Chaplin (whom Stan Laurel once understudied), he did not make an early and complete transition from the theater to the cinema. Instead, he moved back and forth between vaudeville and cinema. But in neither field did he succeed in scaling the heights until he and Oliver Hardy were paired by the Hal Roach Studio. By then, he was already 37 years old. By the time he returned to North Shields for a visit in 1932, he had become an established, international star. But he had been no overnight success. He was then 42 years old.

As well as describing his subsequent successful film career, this book outlines the decline in the fortunes of Laurel and Hardy following Stan's decision to leave the Roach Studio and make films for Twentieth Century–Fox and MGM. After what was, overall, a disappointing experience at these other studios, Stan went back to his first love, the English music hall. Laurel and Hardy embarked on a tour of UK variety theaters in 1947 and received a rapturous reception. Some time after their return to the USA, they received an offer to make a film in France, which must have seemed like a wonderful opportunity for the two now aging comic actors to resume their stalled film careers. Instead, they embarked on a film over which they had little creative control. Filming took much longer than planned. Although the resulting *Atoll K* may have some merit, it was very far from being the international triumph they had hoped. In the course of making it, Stan became seriously ill and underwent surgery, and it was a sick old trouper who returned to the U.S. to ponder what if anything was left for him in the world of entertainment.

After a spell recuperating, he and Oliver Hardy chose to accept two further invitations to make long grueling tours of variety theaters in the UK. On the final tour, both performers developed serious health problems and were forced to abandon their schedule and return to the United States. Neither of them worked in film or theater again. Oliver Hardy died first in 1957. At the time, Stan Laurel was too ill following a stroke to attend his friend and partner's funeral. He did make a reasonable recovery but declined further offers of work and died in 1965 at the age of 74.

1

The Jeffersons

Stan was born into a theatrical family. His father was Arthur Jefferson, a man of many talents. Although described as a comedian on Stan's birth certificate, Louvish insists that this does not mean that Stan's father was a stand-up comedian but rather an actor who specialized in light dramatic roles, as against a tragedian playing parts such as Hamlet or King Lear (Louvish, 2001). There is no doubt that Arthur did play such roles but a surviving photograph of him (see Marriot, 1993 p. 8) with trousers at "half-mast" and a suitcase at his feet identifying him as "Bobby Baxter fra Manchester," suggests that Louvish is too ready to dismiss the description of Arthur as a comedian. The photo may have been taken later in life as Arthur appears to be wearing a wig, and so was probably staged for the camera, but it is still a strong indication that Arthur was a stand-up comedian at some stage in his career. Moreover, the contract he signed with the Roberts, Archer and Bartlett's Royal Standard Dramatic Company in 1883 was to play pantomime at the Theatre Royal in Lincoln. But whatever the roles he played in his earlier career, when he took up a resident position in Ulverston in 1884, it was as actor/manager of the Hippodrome Theatre. It may not have been as grand a theater as its name implies. It was constructed of wood with a canvas roof.[1] However, Spencer's Gaff, as it was known locally, served its purpose for Arthur Jefferson, and by the time that he moved on, he had gained considerable further experience as a manager and playwright as well as player.

It was during this period that Arthur met Stan's mother, Margaret Metcalfe, a draper's saleswoman who preferred to be known as Madge. Arthur is said to have first seen her when she was singing in a church choir. They married on March 19, 1884, at the Holy Trinity Church in Ulverston. Eleven months later, Madge gave birth to their first child, George Gordon Jefferson on February 3, 1885. At this stage in their married life, they were living with

Madge's parents; George (a master shoemaker) and Sarah (née Shaw), just across the road from the Hippodrome which was in Lightburn Park.[2]

Several writers have suggested that Madge's parents were, initially, less than enthusiastic at having a member of the theatrical profession as a son-in-law. If so, Madge must have upset them further by taking up acting herself. She and Arthur moved to County Durham where together they spent a couple of seasons touring with drama companies. Madge appears to have matured into an accomplished actress.

In 1889, Arthur took over the Bishop Auckland Theatre Royal.[3] Shortly afterwards, Madge became pregnant again and she returned to her parents' home to have the baby. (Their address was known as Foundry Cottages according to Owen-Pawson and Mouland but it is described as 3 Foundry Street in the 1891 census and was renamed 3 Argyll Street a few years later.) The decision to have the baby delivered at her parents' home proved to be a wise move. She had a difficult delivery in the back bedroom of the small terraced house on June 16, 1890. The weakly child was not expected to live so arrangements were made for a hurried baptism in the house.[4] But the new baby, Arthur Stanley Jefferson, did not die. He not only survived but grew up to become the red-haired, wonderfully inventive comic actor the world knows as Stan Laurel.

Nevertheless, for the first few years of his life, he needed the kind of care which his mother did not feel she could provide, in part because of a protracted period of ill health following the birth but also because of the character of the theatrical lifestyle which she and Arthur were living. In due course she returned to her husband's side in Bishop Auckland, leaving her baby Arthur Stanley behind in the care of her parents.

It seems inconceivable that Madge would have left her vulnerable child with her parents had her own father George been the chronic drunk and wife beater claimed by Guiles in his portrayal of Stan's early life. His unconvincing account contains tell-tale signs that he was so anxious to suggest parallels in the early life and careers of Charlie Chaplin and Stan Laurel that he went far beyond the normal limits of artistic license. For example, describing George coming home drunk and falling up the "stoop" is unconvincing not least because the simple, terraced house in Ulverston had nothing like an American stoop to fall up.[5] Other accounts describe Madge's parents as Methodists, then the most numerous and influential non-conformists in Britain and a denomination which took a strong stand against alcohol abuse. With a large Wesleyan Methodist church just a very short distance away from the Metcalfe home, Guiles' account becomes even less credible.

Owen-Pawson and Mouland, the local Ulverston writers of *Laurel Before Hardy*, offer no support whatsoever for Guiles' claim. However, they too make a statement about Stan's early life which is difficult to reconcile with the now known facts. They suggest that it was because Stan was such a vulnerable child that "he was the only one of the Jefferson children to stay in Ulverston while the rest of the family travelled" (1984, p. 7). Yet on census night 1891, it was not Arthur Stanley but his elder brother George Gordon who was staying with his grandparents.

On April 5, the day of the census, Stan's parents, Arthur Jefferson (described as a theatrical manager) and his wife Madge were living at 15 High Tenters Street, in a Bishop Auckland lodging house run by the widow Sarah Barker. She may well have been one of those landladies who specialized in theatrical lodgers, who became the butt of so many comedians' jokes, because also staying there at the time was 68-year-old comedian John Price. Boarding next door at number 16 with the Curry family was another theatrical manager, Arthur's business partner Thomas Thore, his actress wife and scenic artist son.

Neither of the Jefferson boys was with his parents at the time. Arthur and Madge's six-year-old son George Gordon was with his grandparents at Foundry Street in Ulverston. However, the nine-month-old Arthur Stanley Jefferson was not listed with his grandparents in Ulverston, his parents in Bishop Auckland, or with his Aunt and Uncle Shaw in Hawes. Searches of both the Ancestry and Findmypast transcriptions of the UK's 1891 census records have so far failed to locate any Arthur or Stanley Jefferson who fits the bill. So, if anyone does know where he was in 1891, please do get in touch!

Despite the fact that George and Sarah may have temporarily mislaid Arthur Stanley in April 1891, or thought it unnecessary to list their grandson on the census return, they did take care of him for the first few years of his life. What is not known is what, if any, contact he had with his Jefferson relatives — or, indeed, precisely who they were.

Arthur Jefferson's parentage remains an unresolved mystery. There are undoubted skeletons in his family cupboard and neither my efforts nor the meticulous research of the genealogist Stella Colwell and family historian Andrew Gough have yet succeeded in producing a robust family tree for him (Colwell, 2003, pp. 264–69; Gough, 2010). It must also be said that none of us has uncovered any evidence to support Gehring's claim that Arthur was related to the British-born American actor Joseph Jefferson or his even more famous grandson Joseph Jefferson III (Gehring, 1990, p. 2). On the contrary, it is probable that Arthur's biological father was not a Jefferson and that Arthur may not have actually understood the complexities of his own family background.

The census records between 1881 and 1901 suggest that he was born about 1862 in either Birmingham or Lichfield (in the vicinity of Birmingham). That is consistent both with a handwritten entry in a family record, which records his birthday as September 12, 1862, and the inscription on his gravestone. All this would indicate that he was about 87 when he died in 1949. Yet his death certificate records his age as 93, and the local newspaper reported his age as 94, suggesting a birth date as early as 1855 or 1856. Because of this, I searched the UK's birth records from 1855 to 1865. Although several entries appeared promising initially, by following up each individual in subsequent census records I was able to establish that none matched the description of Stan Laurel's father. Given his absence from both the index of registered births and the census records for 1861 and 1871, one inevitably wonders if an attempt was being made to conceal his very existence.

It might have been impossible to make further progress had it not been for the careful research of the family historian Andrew Gough.[6] He established that in 1892, two years after Stan's birth, Arthur received a bequest from the will of Col. Alexander Clement Foster Gough, a wealthy Wolverhampton solicitor. A similar bequest was left to Clara Riley, a married woman described as the sister of Arthur Jefferson. Gough's subsequent research into the background of these legacies, to try to establish the nature of the relationship between Arthur and Clara and their benefactor, coupled with my own efforts, have proved most revealing. What they have uncovered is an example of the hypocritical behavior that was commonplace in Victorian England, in which a sordid private life of mistresses and illegitimate children was hidden behind a public facade of middle-class propriety. Alexander Gough may have appeared to be a pillar of his local community: an unmarried professional man who was prominent in his local Masonic

Lodge. The reality is that he enjoyed the company of two and possibly three mistresses and was the father of, or considered himself to be responsible for, at least six children. He left bequests not only to Arthur and Clara but also to the four children of Fanny Morgan, another mistress who (like Arthur's mother) had died before him. In addition, he left a substantial bequest to Bessie King a third close lady friend, who survived him.[7] But, hypocrite or not, it must be to Alexander Gough's credit that he provided so well for them. His £20,000 estate, expressed as the relative share of the UK's GDP for the years 1892 and 2008, would represent over £20 million pounds, or about $30 million based on the exchange rate at the time of writing. If the corresponding dollar figures are expressed in terms of the relative share of the GDP of the USA over the same period, Gough's 1892, $97,000 estate would be worth about $86 million today. Alexander's bequests to his lady friends, and the children for whom he evidently considered himself responsible, made up close to 40 percent of this fortune.[8]

The precise nature of Alexander Gough's relationship with Clara and Arthur we may never know, but there can be no doubt that their mother Harriet (née Wilson) wanted to draw public attention to it. Harriet may have married Christopher Jefferson, a Lichfield grocer, in 1850, and her daughter Clara Wilson may have been registered with that surname the following year, but it is not safe to assume that Christopher Jefferson was her father.[9] On the subsequent 1861 census return, Harriet described her daughter as Clara Gough. She called herself Harriet Gough, although there is no evidence that Christopher had died in the interim or that she had married Alexander. Moreover, two daughters born to Harriet after 1851 were described as Emily Gough and Alice Gough. Proof that Harriet was not satisfied to limit this declaration of her relationship to Alexander Gough to a census document that was to remain confidential for the next 100 years, comes from the fact that, in an 1859 church service, Alice had been christened Alice Foster Gough Gough (i.e., with Gough as a middle name *and* surname). She took similar steps to emphasize the link when two more children were christened in 1861 and 1866. They were christened Mary Ann Foster Gough Gough and William Alexander Gough Gough. The relationship was made even more public and explicit in 1862 when Alice died. Over three days, notices appeared in the *Birmingham Daily Post*, the *Birmingham Daily Gazette* and *Aris's Gazette* to the effect that Alice, the third daughter of Mr. Alexander Gough, solicitor of Wolverhampton, had died on the 13th of May 1862, at Walmer Terrace, Soho Hill, Handsworth.

The implication that Alexander Gough was the father of Harriet's growing family while she remained legally married to Christopher Jefferson must have created particular problems for her in a society in which such illicit relationships were regarded with disapproval. That may help to explain why Harriet seems to have failed to register Arthur's birth at all, but certainly not as either Jefferson or Gough.[10] Who to acknowledge as their father must have also posed a dilemma for Harriet's children as they grew older. What Arthur called himself in his younger years we do not know, but we do know that when he was eight years old he was described as Arthur Gough in the 1871 census return for the Thompson family with whom he was staying. However, in the 1881 census, when he was living independently, he was listed as Arthur Jefferson — suggesting that when free to do so, he had specifically chosen not to follow his mother's example and identify himself with Alexander Gough. That would no doubt have met with the approval of his benefactor, who described Arthur as Arthur Jefferson, actor of Ulverston, in his will and had chosen to identify him as an unrelated beneficiary.

We do not know what kind of relationship Arthur had with Christopher Jefferson. He obviously knew of his existence and described himself as Arthur Jefferson on the 1881 census return and for the rest of his life. However, Harriet's husband has not been located with certainty in the official records after 1851 and it is possible that he may have disappeared from the scene entirely. That Arthur may not have known much about him can also be inferred from the fact that when he married Madge in 1884, he stated that his father was Frank Jefferson, a solicitor. In other words, he conflated the surname of his mother's legal husband with the profession of his probable natural father — and attributed to this invented hybrid an unrelated forename.

Arthur's relationship to Alexander Gough is more firmly established. His mother was obviously keen to put her relationship with him on public record. There is also evidence that Arthur attended Alexander Gough's funeral, and we know that he inherited a very substantial sum of money from him. The relationship is also more interesting and important because Alexander Gough enjoyed connections which may have helped pave the way for Arthur's entry into the theater. In Alexander's will, his legacy to Bessie King was formally described as "to Elizabeth Catherine King, spinster, eldest daughter of my old friend Thomas Charles King, Tragedian." In fact, Thomas Charles King had not just been a distinguished serious actor but also a theater manager and, to give some brief indication of his theatrical stature, he played before Queen Victoria and Prince Albert at Windsor Castle in 1856 and in the role of Othello at the Queen's Theatre Dublin in 1860 when Henry Irving was still a relative unknown playing the supporting role of Cassio. Kathleen (Katty), his younger daughter, followed him onto the stage (as a light comic actress rather than tragedian) and in due course married the influential Arthur Lloyd, the very successful songwriter, composer, playwright and comedian. Lloyd was also a major impresario who ran his own popular theatrical company and was a theater lessee. It seems likely that with his probable biological father Alexander Gough enjoying such a wealth of theatrical connections, Arthur Jefferson may have received help, whether directly or indirectly, with his own theatrical ambitions.[11]

Thanks to a family document which became public for the first time in 2010, we now know that A.J., while living in Manchester, signed a contract with the Royal Standard Dramatic Company in December 1883. Surviving playbills indicate that the Company put on serious as well as lighter productions. Arthur Jefferson was signed to appear in pantomime — at the Theatre Royal at Lincoln which the Company leased between 1880 and 1885. He was paid well, both for his age and for the period. In terms of average earnings, his weekly salary of £1. 10s. would have been the equivalent of about £780 a week (or $1200) in 2010. He received such a relatively generous salary because he played a lead part in the *Babes in the Wood* production which ran for 10 nights from the evening of Boxing Day (26 December) in 1883. The audience participation, which is always a key feature in pantomime, is focused on the villain of the piece. Children are encouraged to boo and hiss his every entry on stage. In the case of *Babes in the Wood*, the villain is the evil Baron, who is intent on killing the babes to secure their inheritance for himself. This heavyweight role is usually played by a strong character with a commanding voice and real stage presence — and is a role often reserved for well-known actors taking a break from the legitimate theatre. In this instance in 1883, the role was played by the young Arthur Jefferson. Despite his age and inexperience, his performance was well-received. The review in the local newspaper described all the artists as "above the average" but added "we must make special mention of..." and amongst those singled out by name was Arthur Jefferson, the Baron (Lincolnshire Chronicle, issue 2844, 28 December 1883 p. 8 col. 3).

If we accept the information on his 1881 Manchester census return, which suggests that Arthur was born in 1864, he would have been just 19 when he signed the contract and played the part. Even if we accept that he was born in 1862, he would have been only 21 years old. Given that he was described as a coal canvasser in 1881, his contract and leading role represents quite a meteoric rise in his fortunes. The contract is a further intimation that, talented though Arthur may have been, he may have had 'friends in the business' to help him become established at such a young age. That is also suggested by the fact that when he took over the Ulverston Hippodrome as its actor/manager he was no more than 22 years old.

The personal and professional network with which Arthur seems likely to have been associated through Alexander Gough is evident in an account of the May 1891 funeral of Katty Lloyd (née King), the younger sister of Alexander's close personal friend Bessie King. The theatrical company with whom Arthur signed his 1883 contract was prominently represented at Katty's funeral. In the obituary in *The Era*, it was recorded that "the coffin was literally smothered with beautiful flowers in baskets, wreathes and crosses, sent by the following professional and private friends." The first listed amongst them was "Messers Archer and Bartlett, Theatre Royal, Croydon." As a close friend of the family, Alexander Gough is likely to have been at the funeral along with Messers Archer and Bartlett and a great many others.

It is the existence of this network, coupled with the timely legacy he received, which makes Arthur's complex family history more than just interesting. It is of particular significance to this book because, had it not been for the relationship and the bequest, Arthur might not have been in a position to establish such an influential role for himself in the theatrical world of the north of England. It was in 1892, shortly after the birth of his son Stanley, that he inherited £500 from Alexander Clement Foster Gough. Today, at a time when bankers are routinely paid bonuses running into millions, £500 (or $2,435 at the then exchange rate) may seem like a paltry inheritance. However, one could do a great deal with such a sum in 1892. In terms of relative share of GDP, it would be worth over £500,000 in 2008 (or about $750,000 at the exchange rate at the time of writing). If expressed in terms of the relative share of the U.S. GDP at the same date, such a legacy would represent about $2.15 million in 2008.

It is not possible to determine exactly how much the legacy helped Arthur to consolidate his theatrical ambitions, but it must have made a significant difference. Whether or not it was appropriate to describe him as a "struggling comedian, actor and writer" when Stan was born in 1890, it is plainly not a fitting description of him after 1892 (Gehring, 1990, p. 1). By then, Arthur (or A.J. as he was becoming known), with the help of his wife Madge, had redesigned the Theatre Royal in Bishop Auckland and re-opened it as the Eden Theatre. In 1893 he re-opened the Theatre Royal in Consett and bought the lease of the Theatre Royal in Blyth (and later had it completely rebuilt). At the time, he also appears to have had more than one touring company traveling around Britain.

On December 16, 1894, there was another addition to the Jefferson family, Beatrice Olga. She was christened on January 3, 1895, at St. Peter's Church in Bishop Auckland. On the same occasion, Arthur Stanley was "received into the Church." It seems probable that by then, Stan had moved from his grandparents' home in Ulverston to become part of his own immediate family.

So, while young Arthur Stanley may have been brought up in a theatrical family, he was certainly not born in the proverbial theatrical trunk or carried from theater to theater, never far from the smell of greasepaint. On the contrary, he was probably brought up for his first four years by his maternal grandparents who seem to have had reservations about their daughter's choice of husband and her decision to follow him onto the stage. Far from spending the evenings of his earliest years in the wings of a theater, Stanley seems to have been brought up in a typically strict English Victorian family, at a time when it was widely believed that children, like the lower classes, should "know their place." Children "should be seen but not heard" when in adult company. The descriptions of Stan's "Granda" locking him in the "wash house" in the backyard when he was naughty, can easily give a misleading impression of his early home life. There is no reason to suppose that this was a case of child abuse. It probably represented nothing more than the Victorian equivalent of the now much favored child development technique of "time-out," in which a boy or girl is isolated in

Map of Britain Showing the Location of Significant Places in the Jeffersons' Family History

Map of Britain showing the location of significant places in the Jeffersons' family history.

a boring place for a short time after he or she has misbehaved. In the small house in Argyll Street, the wash house in the backyard probably served as the equivalent of the "time-out room." Stan seems to have made the best of his spells in it by looking at early versions of comics by candlelight!

The fact that Stanley may have had a typically strict Victorian upbringing in his earliest years does not mean he was not loved by his Metcalfe grandparents. What it does mean is that Stanley must have relished his newfound freedom when he moved from Ulverston to be with his parents, first to Bishop Auckland and then the more exciting, expanding seaport town of North Shields.

2

Stan's Theatrical Inheritance

A.J. took control of the 650-seat Theatre Royal in North Shields in 1895.[1] He was not just a theater manager, as some earlier references to him suggest. On the contrary, he was, in addition to being an already established theater lessee and manager, a talented actor, prolific playwright, consummate showman and entrepreneur. By the time he left the town, he had also become an elected local councilor of the Borough of Tynemouth (of which North Shields was the major part). He had also been accorded public recognition for his charitable work and even had a street named after him in nearby Blyth, alongside the new theater he had built there.[2]

The Jeffersons came to a bustling town, expanding rapidly in size, population and economic development. There was no radio, cinema or television to provide entertainment for its citizens in 1895. Entertainment was live, whether it was amateur or professional, highbrow or lowbrow. It was the theater which dominated the entertainment scene then, just as cinema came to dominate it in the decades that followed until it, in turn, had to cope with the advent of television. The local theatrical scene mattered and it would have been a focal and talking point, commanding attention in much the same way that today's film and television celebrities command attention. The Jeffersons arrived at a time of change, not from the cinema which was still very much in its embryonic form, but because music hall acts and melodrama were becomingly increasingly popular at the expense of the more "legitimate" theater which was aimed primarily at educated, middle-class audiences.

North Shields is located in the northeast of England at the entrance to the River Tyne. Its name derives from the shiels (turf shelters) used by fishermen in its early history. The town grew slowly and haltingly over

600 years before the Jeffersons made their home there in the late 19th century. Its development was thwarted by a long and bitter commercial and political conflict with the burgesses of its much bigger neighbor Newcastle upon Tyne. For most of this period, North Shields struggled to survive in a world of protectionism, dominated not even by national states but by local privileges conferred on towns and cities by royal charters. North Shields was always — and very much — the underdog.[3]

It suffered in many ways as a result of the ruthless domination of the commercial life of the River Tyne by the burgesses of Newcastle. It probably lost most by not being able to share fully in the lucrative trade in coal which meant so much to Newcastle. Coal and Newcastle came to be so closely identified that in many parts of the world, the expression "It's like taking coals to Newcastle" was adopted to signify an activity that was utterly pointless. Had free trade rather than protectionism been the order of the day, the expression might well have been "It's like taking coals to Shields."

Fortunately for North Shields, during the 18th century, demographic, economic and political forces arose in Europe which destroyed the old order. The associated decline in Newcastle's monopolistic position provided commercial opportunities for North Shields' entrepreneurs beyond the dreams of those who had lived in earlier periods. Many became rich and influential in the process, particularly in the key fields of the coal trade, shipping, shipbuilding and fishing.

It was to a still thriving town that the Jeffersons moved during the closing decade of the 19th century. Its economic and physical growth had been spectacular. Originally North Shields was almost entirely limited to a narrow strip of land alongside the river and the adjacent bankside which rose steeply to a plateau about 70 feet (25m) above. The Bank Top (or Bankhead, as it was also known) was free of building until the closing decades of the 18th century. To get to the buildings on the bankside and to the plateau above, a series of steps had been created at intervals running from the riverside. They were narrow and steep and suitable only for those on foot. The only "roads" that led from the Bank Top to the riverside were once described as being so precipitous that they put the lives of both men and horses at risk. As I shall explain in a later chapter, it is not without significance that the Jeffersons' first home in North Shields was in the very first development above the riverside, close to the edge of the Bank Top.

When the Jeffersons arrived in North Shields, it was a lively venue for both low- and highbrow professional theater, something that warrants emphasis, given that North Shields has had no professional theater for the past 75 years. Fortunately, thanks to a study by Robert King, a considerable amount is known about the evolution of North Shields' theaters and it is possible to put A.J.'s theatrical contribution into historical perspective. Quite a lot can be gleaned from King's work about both the nature of the productions and the kind of audiences they attracted before, during and after Stan's father Arthur Jefferson came to dominate it in 1895. It is important to outline the evolution of this local theatrical scene because it was the cultural milieu within which the young Stan Jefferson was socialized and in which he developed his own theatrical ambitions. Living so close to his father's theater and the other theatrical venues in the town, Stan would have enjoyed the company of actors, entertainers and backstage staff of all kinds. They in turn would have enjoyed telling the stage-struck youngster about life on the boards in the good old days. Just as late in life Stan enjoyed reminiscing about the world of theater in the early 20th century, he spent his boyhood rubbing shoulders with men and women who would have enjoyed reminiscing about the world of theater in the 19th century.

North Shields' first theater opened in 1765, at virtually the same time that Stan's first North Shields home was being built on the Bank Top in a development called Dockwray Square. However, the theater was located not on the Bank Top but on the bankside. The proceeds of the first performance went to charity. Such donations from theatrical productions were not uncommon in a seaport where ships and their crews were often lost during bad weather. At other times, performances were given for more general charitable purposes, for example during the "hungry forties," when there was an unusually high level of poverty, and funds were raised for the Victoria Soup Kitchen with reduced price tickets "in order to meet the general distress of the times" (King, 1947, p. 76). That tradition continued right through to Arthur Jefferson's period in the town and beyond. For example, in 1900, the proceeds from the sale of programs in his Theatre Royal were devoted to providing meals for the needy (King, 1948, p. 120).

Moreover, when Laurel and Hardy appeared on the stage of the Gaumont Theatre during their last visit to North Shields in 1952, it was as guests at a charity concert.

The plays presented in the new theater included Shakespeare's *Hamlet* and *The Tempest* and it is noteworthy that serious productions of this kind took place in North Shields throughout the 18th and 19th centuries, long before the advent of compulsory education and at a time when the majority of the population was still illiterate. Sometimes they featured actors with national reputations. Edmund Kean regarded in his day as England's finest actor, performed in North Shields on several occasions while at the peak of his career.[4] In 1885, Oscar Wilde was in North Shields, billed as the *Apostle of Aesthetics*, to give his lecture *The House Beautiful* in which he sought to influence interior house design by encouraging people to give up what he saw as the excesses of the early Victorian period (*Shields Daily News*, November 6, 1885).[5]

In 1785, a new bankside theater was opened by the same company. Access was only possible from the Low Street alongside the riverside. It could not have been pleasant for visitors from a distance to descend down a potentially dangerous road to the Low Street, only to have to climb up the bankside's steep steps, especially on a cold or wet night. Nevertheless, the theater had some influential and enthusiastic patrons, including Lord Delaval who lived five miles away in the impressive Seaton Delaval Hall designed by Sir John Vanbrugh in 1718.[6]

By this time, the development of the Bank Top was well underway. Initially, it was limited to the area in and around Dockwray Square where the Jeffersons were later to take up residence. However, when its owner decided to develop a nearby block of land, the then theater manager James Cawdell took advantage of the opportunity to build a new theater to which, it was emphasized, carriages might be driven close to the doors (King, 1947, pp. 34–35). Although at its opening in 1798 it was claimed that it was "in every respect eligible and commodious both for the town and country," and others described the interior as "handsome and convenient," by 1811 it was said to be as "on too small a scale for a town where the population was advancing so rapidly" (King, 1947, p. 36).[7]

Over the years that followed, the indications are that performances were still targeted at an educated audience. As well as Shakespearean classics and occasional operas (including a touring opera company which performed for six nights in 1866), some performances had a decidedly patriotic and at times jingoistic flavor. Most of the many melodramas of the time tried to combine moral instruction with entertainment. Far from being left implicit, the moralizing was often hammered home in the publicity

---

For the B E N E F IT of poor Widows and
Orphans of Seamen, &e.
At the NEW THEATRE in North Shields,
On FRIDAY Evening next, being the 27th of Sept.
will be presented a celebrated TRAGEDY, call'd

The Diftrefs'd Mother.

PYRRHUS, by Mr WALLACE.
PHOENIX, Mr BLANCHARD.
ORESTES, Mr BRIMYARD.
HERMIONE, Mrs BRIMYARD.
CLEONE, Mrs FITZGERALD.
Preceding the Play, an EULOGIUM on CHARITY,
written by Mr CUNNINGHAM, to be fpoke by
Mrs BRIMYARD.
And between the Play and Farce, a SONG, by
Mr BLANCHARD.
To which will be added a FARCE, call'd

The Spirit of Contradiction.

Mr PARTLET, by Mr BLANCHARD.
Capt. LOVEWELL, Mr WALLACE.
BAT STEER, Mr BRIMYARD.
Mrs PARTLET, Mrs GLENN.
BETTY, Mrs HOLT.
The Profits of this Play will be diftributed at the
Difcretion of feveral Gentlemen of Shields.

Above: Newcastle Evening Chronicle advertisement for the opening of the first documented North Shields theater on September 27, 1765. (From Robert King's 1948 book *North Shields Theatres*.)
Opposite: Theater bill for the appearance of Edmund Kean (1789–1833) at the new North Shields Theatre in 1831. At the time, he was regarded as England's finest Shakespearean actor. (From Robert King's 1948 book *North Shields Theatres*.)

Theatre, North Shields.

THE CELEBRATED MR.

KEAN

During his grand Provincial Tour, is engaged at this Theatre, for One Night only, and will make his appearance on

Wednesday Evening, May 4th, 1831,

When will be presented Shakespeare's Play of the

Merchant

OF

VENICE

The part of Shylock by............Mr. KEAN

Bassanio .... Mr BOOTH	Lorenzo... ...,................... Mr GRAY
Duke of Venice.........Mr LARDNER	Gratiano .... Mr PARRY
Antonio .... Mr YOUNG	Gobbo..........................Mr FULLER
Launcelot Gobbo ....Mr BROOKS	Salanio ....Mr ANTHONY
Tubal ....,.............Mr JONES	Balthaza ....Mr BENSON

Portia ....Mrs PARRY *(late Miss Hargrave)*

Jessica.........................Mrs BOOTH | Narissa ....Miss BLAND

Comic Dance by Mr Lardner.

The whole to conclude with the laughable Musical Farce of the

Weathercock

Tristram Fickle ....Mr PARRY	
Old Fickle..................Mr BROOKS	Briefwit ....Mr FULLER
Sneer ....Mr GRAY	Gardener..................Mr LARDNER
Hairdresser ....Mr BENSON	Servant ....Mr ANTHONY
Variella ....Mrs BOOTH	Ready .... Miss BLAND

☞ NO HALF PRICE.

BOXES—3s.   PIT—2s.   GALLERY—1s.

The Free List, excepting by Purchase, must be suspended.
An early application for Places in the Boxes is earnestly recommended, and to prevent disappointment and confusion, as heretofore, no Seats secured, unless Tickets are taken at the time of entering Names.   The Box Plan is now open as usual, where Tickets and Places may be obtained.

☞ NO ADMITTANCE BEHIND THE SCENES.

T. Hodge, Printer, Sunderland.   Mr. GRAY, Stage-Manager.

for the plays. For example, of *All That Glitters Is Not Gold* the playbill emphasized that "to the humble and lowly it plainly shows that rectitude of conduct and industrious perseverance will never fail to raise them in the estimation of all good men." It continued: "Those who move in the higher circles may learn that Pride and Arrogance, though backed by Riches, may frequently render them objects of ridicule; while kindness and condescension will secure them the love of those whom Fortune has placed beneath them" (King, 1947, p. 88).

There is no doubt that the theater succeeded in drawing "a good class of person" to its productions. In the very first season, the patrons included members of the local Masonic Lodge; Gentleman of the Friendly Club; the Subscribers to the Jerusalem Coffee Room; William Linskill, Esq., and Colonel Lawson de Cardonnel and the Officers of the Northumberland Provisional Cavalry. Similar lists of local worthies survive for later seasons.

After Cawdell's death in 1800, the theater had nine different managers over the next 30 years. It returned to a more stable footing in 1831 when it became part of the Roxby-Beverley partnership, which ran it until 1861. Although the theater was extensively refurbished for the start of the 1839 season and completely rebuilt to a grander design after being destroyed by fire in 1851, its artistic focus seems to have been unchanged. For example, of the 44 performances in the 1839 season, 13 were Shakespearean plays.

After the 1852 re-building, the theater became known as the Theatre Royal. For the first time it was open for six nights a week with a season that ran from October to February with moralizing plays again to the fore. When new management took over from the Roxby-Beverley partnership in 1862, the season was extended from October to April. However, the fortunes of the Theatre Royal began to decline in the decades before the Jefferson family arrived in North Shields, despite an explicit attempt to drum up more business by attracting working class audiences. Music hall-style entertainment was offered in the summer months (with mesmerists, comic and sentimental singers, tumblers, trained dogs and dancers) and

Opposite: A bill for the opening of the first Theatre Royal in North Shields on November 8, 1852, at the junction of Howard Street and Union Street. (From Robert King's 1948 book *North Shields Theatres.*)

Theatre Royal, **North Shields.**

GRAND OPENING NIGHT.

PROPRIETOR & MANAGER, Mr. SAMUEL ROXBY.

ARCHITECT, Mr. G. A. MIDDLEMISS.

THE MAGNIFICENT NEW ACT DROP BY

Mr. WILLIAM BEVERLY.

The whole of the Interior Paintings, Decorations and splendid New Scenery by

Mr. PERCIVAL C. SIMMS.

Monday Evening, 8th Nov., **1852,**

AN INTRODUCTORY ADDRESS will be delivered by

Mr. ROXBY,

Previous to the Grand National Anthem of

GOD SAVE THE QUEEN,

BY THE WHOLE COMPANY,

After which, will be produced, never before acted in Shields, a New Comic Drama, in Three Acts, called

THE PRIDE OF THE MARKET

Marquis de Volange,.... Mr LEANDER MELVILLE—Baron Troptard, Mr C. H. SIMMS,
Chevalier de Bellerive, Mr MILNES LEVICK—Ravenne, Mr G. BALL—Dubois, Mr BRIDGMAN,
Isadore Parine, ... Mr S. CALHAEM—Ravel, ... Mr DOWNEY.
Pierre, ... Mr BENSON—Fontaine, ... Mr F. CALHAEM.
Madlle. de Volange,........ Miss HENRIETTA SIMMS—Manton, ... Miss ELY LOVEDAY,
Javotie, Mrs C. H. SIMMS—Annette, Miss ELLEN PEEL—Louison, Miss FANNY ROBERTSON,
Madelon,...... .... Miss E. ROBERTSON—Elise,...... Mrs RICKARDS,
Claribel, ... Mrs USHER—Faaebette, ... Miss MURRAY.

NEW SCENERY:

Act 1st.—GRAND MARKET PLACE IN PARIS.

ACT 2nd.—MAGNIFICENT SALOON IN THE PALACE OF THE MARQUIS DE VOLANGE.

Act 3rd.—Royal Gardens in Paris.

Painted by Mr. PERCIVAL C. SIMMS.

To which will be added, an Entire NEW INTERLUDE, called the

QUEEN'S HORSE;

Or, the BREWER OF PRESTON.

Tom Tubbs, the Brewer of Preston, Mr HARRY BEVERLY—Captain Forecastle, Mr MILNES LEVICK,
Adjutant, Mr BRIDGMAN—Corporal Murphy, Mr LEANDER MELVILLE.
Sam, Mr S. CALHAEM—1st Brewer, Mr F. CALHAEM—2nd Ditto, Mr DOWNEY—3rd Ditto, Mr G. BALL.
1st Soldier, Mr GILBERT—2nd Ditto Mr CATTLE.
Mary Wakefield, Miss HENRIETTA SIMMS—Susan, Miss ELLEN PEEL—Kate, Miss F. ROBERTSON,
Nelly, Miss E. ROBERTSON—Sally, Miss MURRAY—Maud, Mrs USHER—Dolly, Mrs RICKARDS.

The unequalled **NEW ACT DROP**, painted expressly for this occasion by

Mr. WILLIAM BEVERLY,

The acknowledged First Scenic Artist in the World, will be exhibited during the Performances.

THE SPLENDID NEW BAND,

Will perform, during the Evening, several Overtures, Polkas, Valtzes &c., led by **Mr WICKETTS**
From the Royal Italian Opera House, London.

The whole to conclude with Planche's Fashionable Farce called, THE

PRINTER'S DEVIL

Or, the Proclamation.

Count de Maurepas, ... Mr LEANDER MELVILLE—Duke de Brioghen,...... Mr BRIDGMAN,
Gniffet, Mr M. LEVICK—Justin, Mr F. CALHAEM—Pierre Pica, the Printer's Devil, Mr ROXBY.
Madame Girard, Mrs BANKS BALL—Cecile, Miss E. ROBERTSON.

The Doors will be open at Half-past Six, Performance to commence at Seven o'Clock.

BOXES 2s.—PIT 1s.—GALLERY 6d.

Half-price to the BOXES only, at NINE O'CLOCK. No admittance behind the Scenes. No Smoking
allowed in any part of the Theatre. Children in arms cannot be admitted

Notice.—As a single glance will convince all Visitors to the Theatre of the immense outlay of Capital, it
is humbly and respectfully hoped, by the Proprietor, that all Persons will refrain from touching any part of
the Decorations with their hands.
Any Person throwing anything into the Pit or on the Stage, or using bad language, and whistling, or other
unseemly noises, interruptions of the performance, and annoyance to the audience, will immediately be taken into
custody by the Police Officers appointed for that purpose, ejected from the Theatre, and no money returned.
Places for the Boxes may be secured at Messrs. Philipson & Hare's, Booksellers, Tyne Street, where the
Box Plan now lies. Stage Manager, Mr. HARRY BEVERLY. Manager, Mr SAMUEL ROXBY, 67,
Stephenson Street, North Shields. [*Vivat Regina*]

PHILIPSON & HARE, PRINTERS NORTH SHIELDS

in advertisements the theater was dubbed The People's Hall and The People's Home. It was all to no avail and the original Theatre Royal closed in 1876.

A few years earlier, Samuel Chisholm had opened the Northumberland Music Hall not far from the Theatre Royal on the west side of Borough Road. Surprisingly, King does not seem to have considered that competition from this lighter alternative form of entertainment might have contributed to the Theatre Royal's demise but it cannot be a coincidence that, when it closed in 1876, a theatrical license was sought for the Music Hall. The application was refused by local magistrates on the grounds that the wooden building was not structurally suitable for a theater. That appears to have been a sound judgment. The roof collapsed under the weight of heavy snow in 1878 and the building was damaged beyond economic repair. It is an indication of the popularity of music hall entertainment at the time that a subscription was raised in the town on behalf of the proprietor. He hired a nearby hall and provided entertainment there until Chisholm's Grand Theatre of Varieties, with 650 seats, was opened in Prudhoe Street in December 1879 (King, 1947, p. 106). It is interesting that, though a permanent building, it was built in the form of a traveling theatrical booth (i.e., with a platform jutting onto the street where the performers could be seen before the show and a showman could draw attention to their talents in an attempt to drum up an audience).

Such traveling booths, made of wood and canvas, had been visiting North Shields since at least the early part of the 19th century and probably much earlier. They usually had a fairground or circus character, or featured animals, such as the famous Wombwell's Menagerie. However some did offer their audiences plays as well as other forms of entertainment. Many successful actors in the regular theater began their careers in the booths, while some once-successful regular theater actors ended their careers in them. They offered a more sensational and sentimental type of performance than that available at the more legitimate Theatre Royal.

In 1882, Chisholm's Grand Theatre of Varieties changed direction. Perhaps in response to competition from the George Tavern (which was to become the Alexander Music Hall and later Siddall's) on King Street, and the similar entertainment offered in the Star and Garter on Clive Street, variety was ditched in favor of legitimate theater. At about the same

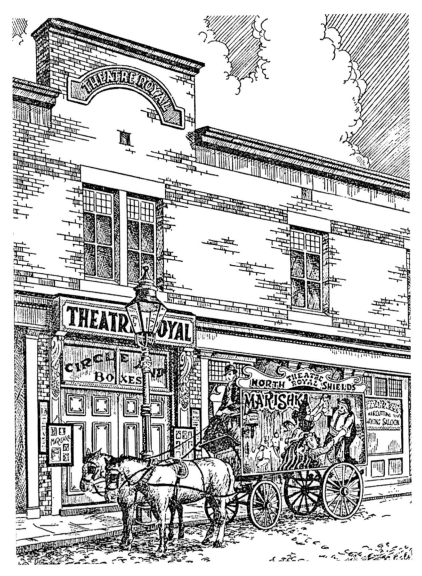

Norman Darling's drawing of the new Theatre Royal in Prudhoe Street, North Shields, in 1884, shortly before it was taken over by Arthur Jefferson. Note the lurid advertising hoarding for the artiste or play *Marishka* on the side of the carriage and the coal gas street lamp. A modest glass and metal awning was later fitted over the main entrance. (From Robert King's 1948 book *North Shields Theatres*.)

time, the promenade in front of the building was replaced with a porch and a new (or rather old) name adopted: the Theatre Royal. A little later, a decorative canopy was added to make the entrance more obvious and afford a little protection against the weather for those patrons waiting for their carriages to arrive to collect them.

The entertainment was still generally of a more popular kind than that which had been available at the original Theatre Royal. From time to time there were Shakespearean plays and performances by actors of national standing, such as Osmond Tearle, but on the whole, the productions appear to have been much less serious and what some fans of Tearle dubbed "sensational trash" (King, 1947, p. 114).[8] Obvious examples of what they had in mind were "a new and original burlesque" entitled *The Ill-Fated Isabel That Was a Belle* and *Romeo the Radical and Juliet the Jingo*.

A photograph (circa 1909) of the Theatre Royal in North Shield, as it looked when it was being leased by Arthur Jefferson. The boy leaning against the Pit entrance in the cap and Eton collar is unknown but a few years earlier the young Stanley Jefferson could well have been seen standing in the same position. (Courtesy of North Tyneside Local Studies Library.)

In 1895, Chisholm retired and the lease was transferred to Arthur Jefferson. He had already appeared at the Theatre Royal as an actor and playwright, first in the early 1890s and then again in 1895. On both occasions he and his wife Madge had appeared in Jefferson's own play *The World's Verdict*. The local theater critic had been particularly impressed by the special effects: "The maniac's den and the knife descended upon his victim by a marvelous piece of mechanism.... To make the scene of Hazelwood Farm more realistic, pigeons, ducks and rabbits are introduced" (King, 1948, p. 118).

The first production at the Theatre Royal under Jefferson was on August 17, 1895 when he presented Edmund Tearle's (Osmond's brother's) company in the usual repertoire of Shakespearean and costume plays (*Shields Daily News*, August 17, 1895). His own melodrama *The Orphan Heiress* was very well received in December. The play was described as "sensational" and its big scene *The Cage of Death* took place in a circus (King, 1948, p. 119). The *Shields Daily News* review was most enthusiastic — not least about the performances of Jefferson himself and his wife Madge:

> Last night the house at Mr. Jefferson's cosy theater was crowded in every part to witness a new production by the popular lessee, entitled *The Orphan Heiress*. Mr. Jefferson himself undertakes one of the characters, that of "Ginger," and is responsible for most of the fun. His eccentricities and comicalities were very entertaining, and appealed to the risible faculties of the audience. We also see Mrs. Jefferson (Madge Metcalfe — a Shields favourite) prominent in the case, and she proved herself an able exponent of the part allotted to her.

In 1931, the editor of the *Shields Hustler* newspaper recalled the impression the *Cage of Death* scene had made on him:

> In one scene there were three cages on stage; in the left one there was a panther, and the right one contained a bear. The central cage was empty. The villain thrust the heroine into the centre cage, and then pulled away the division so that the panther could spring through and devour her, but the "bear" promptly opened his division and pulled her to safety. The "bear" was Mr. Jefferson, of course, playing the low comedy part, in which he used to excel.
>
> On the first night excitement was at fever heat, and two eminent townsmen, with their wives, and some members of their families, were in the left-hand box. When the heroine was thrust into the cage it was too much

for one of the gentlemen, who yelled, "You blackguard!" at the villain, and proceeded to climb out of the box onto the stage, having to be restrained by a friend who was hanging on to his coat tails. I was present and witnessed the incident, which caused intense amusement. The "panther" was a trained dog.

The full, inside story of the opening night was then revealed by no less a person than A.J. himself in a subsequent letter to the Editor.

I had a hearty laugh over your recollection of [the] *Orphan Heiress* play incident. I remember it quite well! Yes, the "panther" was a dog (Great Dane) enveloped in a skin, and proved a very effective substitute. Originally, the play was licensed with the appearance of the real animal but, at the last moment, a bombshell was launched from the Lord Chamberlain's office in the shape of a withdrawal of the consent.... As the tour was booked, and production close at hand, I was at my wit's end on how to cope with the situation. Then the idea of the dog and a skin came, and then the troubles began! ... All went well until the night of the dress rehearsal.... Everything then went and promised well until the *Cage of Death* scene — upon the success of which the play practically depended.... When the two men started to scrap, Mr. Panther let forth the most thunderous volume of barking I have ever heard, and in trying to get at the combatants hurled itself against the bars and practically wrecked its skin! Consternation! Sack-cloth and ashes! And every other ingredient of the mixture known as pessimism veiled the air.... Then another inspiration. Teach him not to bark; and with the aid of a muzzle ... I persuaded him that the two gentlemen were only playing and that it was rude to bark! You can guess the fearful anticipation when the actual scene was displayed to a crowded house ... but having made a hole in the canvass part of the cage, from which he could see me and hear my subdued voice ... all went well and thunders of applause, plus several curtains, proclaimed we had done the trick.

The following December, Jefferson put on a copyright production of another of his own melodramas. Originally called *The Bootblack* when it premiered in North Shields, it was later revised and toured successfully for many years as *London by Day and Night* (King, 1948, pp. 119–20).

Stan recalled that his father was an adept showman when it came to advertising the performances at his Theatre Royal. In one stunt he arranged for a lion in a cage to be mounted on a wagon and hauled through the streets. Inside the cage was a dummy dressed to look like a man and inside the dummy was a big piece of meat to ensure that the lion would look as if it was devouring the body. As crowds gathered around the cage, a canvas sign would drop down reading **Tonight at the Theatre Royal!**

Another stunt was to have a hansom cab driving around with a chap in evening dress, seemingly dead, with a dagger in his chest, bleeding heavily, and the cabby unaware of the situation. This would be advertising a horror show. Or once in a while, Dad would have a balloon released and, at a certain height, smoke would come out, people would gather and then a big advertising banner would drop out and hang there [Stan Laurel quoted by McCabe, 1976, pp. 15–16].

As these advertising stunts would suggest, the staple fare at the new Theatre Royal was primarily melodrama; Jefferson's showmanship extended to what was seen inside the theater as well as the way his productions were advertised outside. Instead of relying on simple painted backdrops, he portrayed sensational incidents, often involving the use of elaborate special effects, and his advertisements drew particular attention to them. One assumes that the audiences of the day did not take his advertising claims literally because they proclaimed "a bridge blown to pieces; a dive to death on horseback; a fast train picking up mails at 40 mph; the Indian Ghost dance that caused the late insurrection in North America and a great race with blood horses" (King, 1948, p. 119). The diet of melodrama was supplemented with musical comedy and some "better class plays," such as those presented by Mrs. Bandman-Palmers Company and the Shakespearean Tearle Company which still made an almost annual visit. But, in 1897, as an indication of the changes to come, "cinematograph" films about 15 minutes long were shown for the first time before the start of the live performance. At the time they were variously described as "animated photographs," "living pictures" and "the New American Bioscope" (King, 1947, p. 120).

Arthur Jefferson claimed in a 1932 interview with a reporter from the magazine *Picturegoer*, that he was the first to introduce cinema to the north of England. Whether or not this particular claim is warranted, there is no doubt that Arthur was a pioneer.[9] There is firm evidence that he was using Poole's Myriorama, "The New and Improved Cinematograph," at his Blyth Theatre Royal in April 1900 and he may have introduced it to North Shields even earlier, in February 1899 (*Shields Daily News*, February 7, 1899). He also seems to have brought something still more advanced to his North Shields Theatre Royal a few months later.

I went up to London and while there I met a Mr. Walter Gibbons — now Sir. And he showed me a marvelous appliance that would project living, moving pictures onto a screen. He called it the Randvoll and, having seen the miracles he had described to me with my own eyes, I bought it. And so it came about that I took the first kinema projector to the North.

The *Shields Daily News* in January 1901 contained the following advertisement for a special New Year attraction as an accompaniment to the usual play.

> Living pictures by the Royal Randvoll. A thousand feet of Film. New subjects will be shown, including the most marvelous Film of the present day, specially recorded for the Holiday Season, and the first duplicate secured for the provinces, entitled *The Children's Dream of Christmas — In Ye Olden Times* (20 scenes). (Louvish, 2001, p. 19).

A.J. was asked in 1932 both how his audiences and his son Stan reacted to the innovation.

> And did the North like it? "Not a bit: not even when I put a singer at the back and tried to synchronise her with the film." And did Stan get excited? "Not a bit. I don't remember a single display of enthusiasm on his part. In that black box lay his future fortunes. And he was not even interested. I sold it in the end for a trifle to a man with whom I was having a drink. He started in the moving-picture business with it. To-day he is a leading film magnate, but I shan't hint at his identity, except to say that I sometimes see him arriving at his office in Wardour Street in his Rolls-Royce" [Stan Laurel Correspondence Archive project website].

Jefferson, always the entrepreneur and showman, tried other innovations while at the Theatre Royal. In October 1898 he announced a scheme to insure all patrons who bought programs (against what is not clear). Then in January 1899, a notice was issued: "The lessee begs to notify patrons that he has entered into an arrangement with the National Telephone Company so that subscribers so desirous can be placed in direct communication with the stage and listen to the performance" (King, 1948, p. 120). This early attempt at broadcasting can only have been intended as a publicity stunt — or as means of Arthur Jefferson keeping tabs on his performers from home. He certainly could not have anticipated that it would provide the theater with a significant new income stream. My research indicates that at the time there were only 77 National Telephone Company lines installed in the whole of North Shields and no more than a further 12 in nearby Tynemouth and Whitley Bay. Jefferson himself had two of the lines (one at the theater and another at home) and most of the rest were registered to businesses (Ancestry, 2010).

2. Stan's Theatrical Inheritance

When Jefferson's lease on the Theatre Royal ran out in 1902, he could not agree terms on a renewal and it was taken over by L.M. Snowdon, who was already the lessee of the South Shields Theatre Royal. Jefferson then concentrated his attention on the nearby Boro (short for Borough) Theatre (on the Ropery Bank at the bottom of Rudyard Street) which he also owned or controlled. This wooden building had been run as a permanent ring circus for a short time by Henry Alvo Thorpe (as Alvo's Circus). It opened on Christmas Eve 1900 but when Thorpe died in March 1901, Jefferson reopened it as the Boro' of Tynemouth Circus and Novelty Hippodrome. He then refurbished it and it re-opened in July 1902 as the Borough Theatre. The Boro' under Jefferson and the Theatre Royal under Snowdon put on similar performances and there was a conspicuous rivalry between them but, of the two, the Boro' seems to have had "a greater proportion of good plays and players" (King, 1948, p. 121). Jefferson also appears to have won the war of words between them. For example, when the Theatre Royal was re-opened after renovation in 1903, Jefferson was quick to point out that the work had been done by firms from outside North Shields, whereas the Boro' had been built by Boro' [i.e., Borough of Tynemouth] tradesmen, furnished by Boro' tradesmen and was "liberally patronized by Boro' inhabitants." He boasted that 160,080 people had paid for admission during his first season.

After months of wrangling, Jefferson regained control of the Theatre Royal in 1904 and re-opened it on September 5. In December, it again hosted the prestigious Osmond Tearle Shakespearean and Classical Repertoire Company. Jefferson's association with the Boro' continued in tandem but he tried to ensure that it would no longer be in direct competition with the Theatre Royal by re-opening it as a Theatre of Varieties. However, it was not a propitious time to do so because by then, the Central Palace of Varieties had opened on Saville Street and music hall entertainment was available in a number of other smaller venues in the town. Although Jefferson's Theatre of Varieties closed within months, it later became the cradle for an even more successful theatrical and cinematic empire. After the Jeffersons left the town, it was taken over by the Black family. They went on to found a large national theater corporation which merged with Moss Empires in 1932, earning George Black the nickname "Emperor of Variety."[10]

At this stage, Arthur Jefferson's theatrical empire was at its height. In North Shields, he was lessee of the Borough of Tynemouth Theatre of Varieties, the Theatre Royal and the Albion Assembly Rooms (at the junction of Norfolk Street and Charlotte Street opposite the Town Hall). He also held leases on the Theatre Royals of Blyth (rebuilt and re-opened in 1900), Wallsend and Hebburn. Then in 1901 it was announced that he had also taken over the Metropole Theatre in Glasgow (*Shields Daily News*, July 1, 1901). He left it in the hands of an acting manager for some years and continued to run his empire from North Shields. However, in 1905, for reasons that remain uncertain, the whole Jefferson family left the town and went to live in Glasgow. Arthur continued with his lease of the Theatre Royal until July 1907 when he transferred it to Stanley Rogers.

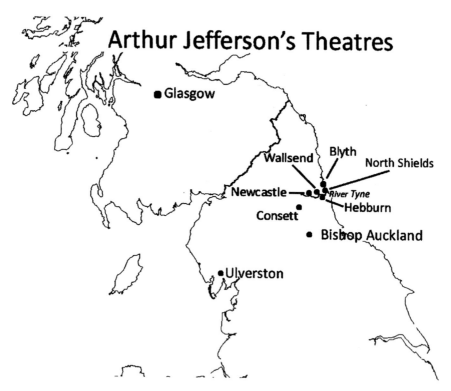

Map of the north of England and Scotland showing the locations of Arthur Jefferson's theaters.

Glasgow Metropole notice (circa 1901), describing Arthur Jefferson as the lessee and manager of not only the Metropole but also the Theatre Royals of North Shields, Blyth, Wallsend and Hebburn and the Boro' of Tynemouth Circus at North Shields.

By then, there are indications that the Theatre Royal was beginning to struggle and the cinema was already beginning to have an impact on live theater. The Boro' had given up on music hall programs and become a "picture house." The Howard Hall and the Albion (in which Arthur Jefferson had an interest) were also showing films on a regular basis.[11]

In its final decades, after Jefferson moved on, the productions on offer at the Theatre Royal seem to have been increasingly sensational or sentimental, e.g. *White Slaves, Tainted Goods, The Apple of Eden, A Warning to Women, No Mother to Guide Her* and *Salome, the Dancing Girl of Galilee*. A spate of war plays were also produced (and presumably specially written) for the period from 1914 to 1918. They included *In Time of War, The Women in Khaki, His Mother's Rosary, Brave Women Who Wait* and *The Munition Girl's Love Story*. In the final eight years of its existence, the theater concentrated on revue and pantomime with only occasional drama.

The Theatre Royal continued in business until 1932. Plans were drawn up in 1933 to demolish and replace it with the Cinema Royale, which would have also had a variety stage. However, the project came to nothing and on August 22, 1939, the *Shields Evening News* carried a photograph of the Theatre Royal along with the caption "The Old Theatre Royal in Prudhoe Street, North Shields, which will shortly be disappearing under a demolition scheme."[12]

It is ironic that competition from the increasingly popular cinema may have been a factor in the Jeffersons leaving North Shields and that young Stanley, who by then had ambitions to go on the boards himself as a comedian, was to have his greatest success not in the theater but in the cinema as a writer, director and comic actor in Hollywood. He was to return to the theater only when, in his late 50s, his film career was in decline.

3

Family Life in North Shields

It is not possible to make a definitive statement on when the Jefferson family moved to North Shields. King's research into North Shields' theaters revealed that A.J. and Madge visited the town at least twice in 1890 and that A.J.'s theatrical company performed his own plays at the Theatre Royal in that year. In a public meeting in 1901, A.J. announced that he had been living in the town for seven years, suggesting an arrival date of 1894. However, because his daughter Beatrice was baptized in Bishop Auckland in January 1895, there is reason to suppose that his family may not have joined him at that stage. What we do know is that he was in control of the Theatre Royal in 1895 so it seems reasonable to suppose that his family could have joined him later in that year. That is consistent with A.J. first appearing on the electoral register at 8 Dockwray Square in October 1897. Registration then, as now, took place at a specified date each year. Given the required 12-month residential period, his appearance on the register indicates that he was definitely a resident of North Shields by July 15, 1896, but could have become a resident any time between July 16, 1895, and July 15, 1896.[1]

Initially, the Jeffersons lived in 8 Dockwray Square, an iconic North Shields' address. It had the distinction of being part of the first residential plot to be developed on the Bank Top above the riverside town in 1763. Before then, North Shields had been physically limited to the narrow strip of land that ran alongside the river close to the entrance to the Tyne.

The long narrow street and the plateau above were originally virtually separate worlds. The inhabitants of North Shields, almost all of whom before the town's expansion earned their living directly or indirectly from activities related to the river and sea, were crammed into the squalid, unsanitary buildings packed tightly together in courts leading off the Low Street, on quays resting on piles driven into the bed of the river, or in dwellings built into the steep bank rising from the river. The Bank Top was used as pasture for cattle.

Originally owned by Tynemouth Priory, the land on the Bank Top had passed through several hands after the dissolution of the monasteries in 1539, until it became the property of Algernon, the 10th Earl of Northumberland. His initial attempts to persuade his local tenants to consent to the "enclosure" of the common land failed but, in 1649, they finally agreed. Over a century later, the 20 acres allocated to John Carruth eventually came into the possession of Thomas Dockwray, the vicar of Stamfordham, a parish about 20 miles west of North Shields.[2]

The Rev. Thomas Dockwray has been described as the founder of the modern town of North Shields because, in 1763, he initiated the building of squares and streets on his land on the Bank Top. Dockwray Square came first — with the south side left undeveloped to retain a view over the river.[3] After his death, Dockwray's representatives built on the remainder of his land. Dockwray's example was soon followed by the other freeholders. The result was that the land on the Bank Top immediately above the North Shields Low Street became effectively part of North Shields. These new developments were a mixture of private dwelling houses and public buildings but Dockwray Square itself was made up of only elegant, terraced houses.

Although housing developments such as Dockwray Square provided superior housing for those with money and high social status, their residents could not avoid all the repercussions of the economic activity and the squalor of the life of the ordinary people who lived just below them. Indeed, according to the Ranger Report of 1851, the area in and around Dockwray Square, which had not been developed until the closing decades of the 18th century, was already being abandoned in the 1840s by those who could afford to live elsewhere.

So, although 8 Dockwray Square is usually considered to have been a rather grand address when young Arthur Stanley Jefferson lived there, the truth is that Dockwray Square had already become a mixed neighborhood. The previous long-standing occupant of number 8 had been Richard Irvin, one of the town's leading citizens and most successful businessmen.

Aerial photograph of the area around Stan Laurel's 8 Dockwray Square boyhood home, taken shortly after his 1932 visit. Almost all the "unfit for human habitation" bankside houses, which had still been standing during his visit, had been demolished by the time this photograph was taken. In other respects, the area was largely unchanged. The image also shows the location of three of the many steep flights of stairs which will be mentioned in Chapter 7. (Courtesy of North Tyneside Local Studies Library.)

However, it is obvious from the occupations of the Jeffersons' neighbors that by the time Irvin moved out and the Jeffersons moved in, there had already been a downward trend at work in terms of the social status of the Square's residents. At number 1, there were three separate households headed by "workers" (a steam engine fitter, a coachman in a livery stable and a coach painter). Number 2, in contrast, was still in single occupation. The head of that household was a self-employed sea-pilot who lived with two sons (one a solicitor) and a domestic servant. Next door, at number 3, lived a railway inspector in a household without a servant. The chief constable lived at number 4 and a surgeon at number 5. Both households had domestic servants. The head of the household of number 6, however, had a more modest occupation. A draper's assistant, he lived there with his wife, four daughters and two sons — but it is indicative of the times that even this family enjoyed the services of a domestic servant.

Number 8, the Jeffersons' residence, was flanked by two lodging or boarding houses. At number 7 lived a widow with three daughters (one a confectioner's shop assistant), a son (an ironmonger's clerk) and a solitary boarder (an electrical engineer). At number 9, another widow, with a son and two daughters, had five boarders to supplement her income (two journalists and three traveling drapers).

The 1901 census entry for 8 Dockwray Square is interesting for several reasons. The first is that Arthur Stanley's sister Beatrice was not with the family. Despite being only six years old, she appears to have been a boarder at St. Mary's Boarding School in Berwick on Tweed (65 miles to the north on the border between England and Scotland). Of the 16 students listed on census night, Beatrice was much the youngest. The oldest was 18 and the average age was 14.25. The nearest girl in age to Beatrice was 11. The second reason the entry is interesting is that it reveals that Arthur Stanley and George Gordon were by then known by their middle rather than first names — and for this reason Arthur Stanley will only be referred to as Stanley or Stan from this point on.

It also indicates that something special was happening in the Jefferson household on that 1901 census night of March 31. Arthur, Madge and their sons Gordon and Stanley were at home along with two general domestic servants. Madge's mother Sarah was also with them. However, it is the addition of Mary Ellis to the list which gives us the clue to what was going on. Mary is described as a "monthly nurse" and, as an article in *The Nursing Record* for May 21, 1891, explains, a monthly nurse was a midwife for home births. In short, Madge was pregnant again and giving birth on census night. As the completed census record shows, at 3.45 am on April 1, 1901, she gave birth to a son, who was recorded without a name. But, presumably because the baby had not actually emerged by midnight, his entry was subsequently crossed out: a wonderful example of bureaucratic pedantry. The same zealous official appears to have spotted that Arthur's birth was recorded as Lichfield, Warwickshire, and corrected it to Staffordshire. The baby was later named Edward (Teddy) Everitt. The successful birth must have been a relief to the family because just two years earlier, on April 30,

1899, another son, Sydney Everitt, had been born but had died just five months later on September 10.[4]

With the exception of Teddy, all the Jefferson children grew up to have what their father described as an "enamorment of the stage" and they followed their parents into the world of theater. Gordon went on to become a theater manager in his own right and was able to help Stan out in 1912 when he was having a rough time. He died in 1938. After a further spell of education in a Belgium convent, Beatrice Olga married William Woods in 1921. She continued to tour as an actress but eventually retired from the stage after a second marriage to William Healey. Although she lived in the Midlands for many years, she chose to retire to the northeast of England and died in Roker, near Sunderland, at age 81 in 1976. Stan, of course, served his apprenticeship in the English and Scottish music halls before going on to become an international film star. Teddy alone was not interested in the theater. His love was cars. The nearest he got to the theater or cinema was working as Stan's chauffeur for many years. He died tragically in 1933 as a result of complications following dental surgery.

Although Arthur Jefferson is remembered most for his theatrical contributions to the life of North Shields and the surrounding areas in which he had theatrical interests, he was also an elected local councilor and philanthropist. He was elected in 1901 for a large constituency which included the adjacent villages of Tynemouth and Cullercoats. Although his opponent lived in the ward, the well-known Arthur Jefferson defeated him comfortably, 833 votes to 661. He served for several years until he moved away to Glasgow.

During his time in North Shields, A.J. and his wife Madge were also very active in charitable work and they played a full part in the social life of the town. Stan recalled that his father even arranged special matinee performances for those in the local workhouse and gave them packages of what were then luxuries, such as tea, sugar, biscuits and tobacco as they were leaving the theater (Stan Laurel quoted by McCabe, 1976, p. 16). His parents' generosity was recognized publicly on several occasions as is evident by a scrutiny of the archives of the local newspapers of the period. For example, a presentation was made to both A.J. and his wife in September 1902 for their charitable work. Just weeks later, A.J. received a presentation from the Trades and Friendly Societies of the town (*Shields*

Daily News, September 25, 1902, and October 3, 1902). A similar presentation was made in Wallsend (where A.J. had another theater) at a dinner held in his honor in 1902. "The object of the gathering was an expression of the gratitude of the inhabitants of Wallsend for the many kindly acts he had performed since he came to the Borough, often lending the theater and giving general support to any charitable scheme that was set afloat in the town" (*Wallsend Herald*, January 24, 1902).

When the *Tyneside Weekly News* reported the tragic early death of Madge in December 1908, the whole of the second paragraph of the obituary was devoted to her charitable work:

> During the years Mr. Jefferson resided in North Shields, his wife became particularly well known. She and her husband, both open-hearted and generous almost to a fault, spent a considerable amount of money amongst the poor people of the town. It will probably be never known how much they spent upon food and clothing for the distressed. For the children they had particularly warm affection, and they must have distributed hundreds of pairs of boots and shoes to cover little cold feet. When the South African

The commanding view to the east which Stan enjoyed as a boy from Dockwray Square, over the Fish Quay below; the entrance to the River Tyne; the North and South Shields piers and the North Sea beyond. (Courtesy of North Tyneside Local Studies Library.)

War was going on, they were active in their support of the local Reservist's Fund, and when, towards the close of hostilities, the people had occasion to rejoice at the taking of Pretoria, or the relief of Mafeking, they joined vigorously in the jubilations. In fact, some of their admirers presented them with an illuminated address in recognition of their organizing abilities in connection with one patriotic demonstration [*Tyneside Weekly News*, December 11, 1908].

It has been suggested that living in Dockwray Square, at the entrance to the Tyne, with its commanding views of both the river and North Sea, helped give Stan his lifelong love of the sea. If that is so, it could have been a disappointment when he learned around 1902 that the family was moving from Dockwray Square to Ayton House, at the northern end of Ayre's Terrace, which stood much closer to a local graveyard than the river and sea. Even so, Stan's new house was little more than half a mile from Dockwray Square and the riverside and a little closer to the home of his lifelong friend Roland Park in Northumberland Square. Moreover, as will be explained in the next chapter, his father provided him with something in the larger Ayton House that would not have been possible in Dockwray Square.[5]

4

Boyhood Years

Stan lived in North Shields from about 1895 to 1905, a period he described as the happiest in his life. At that time, the busy town was probably at the height of its economic fortunes although certainly not yet at the limit of its physical expansion.

The images that follow give some indication of how North Shields would have looked to him as he walked from his father's Theatre Royal in Prudhoe Street, along Saville and Charlotte Streets to his home in Dockwray Square. Taking that route after 1901, he would have walked alongside double-decker electric trams and the high ornate standards which carried their cables all the way down to the New Quay ferry landing by the river's edge. Shortly after crossing a steep road down to the river he would no doubt have stopped to look at what was on offer that week at the Central Palace of Varieties, a new venture that had opened in 1901. On his way home he would have looked into the windows of the numerous thriving shops and, let's hope, at his tender age of 11, hurried past the many bars, all with their own distinctive tiled decorations. He may have looked at who was preaching at the large imposing Primitive Methodist Church that coming Sunday (on a site later occupied by Woolworth's until 2009) and then been grateful that living in Dockwray Square meant that he did not need to use the facilities of the Public Baths which he passed a short time later. He may have called into the Public Library on Howard Street to borrow a book or read the day's newspapers. Had he glanced up and down that street he would have seen an array of four churches and other fine buildings up towards Northumberland Square, and an equally impressive array of buildings down towards the river. The imposing John Dobson–designed Town Hall and Magistrates Court came next, across the road from the Albion Assembly Rooms (where he was to be wined and dined on his return in 1932).

Closer to home, he would have passed the main post office, an indoor market and many more shops before he climbed the steps to number 8 Dockwray Square.

The fact that these photographs will not look familiar to those who today live in or visit the town of North Shields, is due in large measure to conscious decisions taken by its elected councilors and local officials just a few years after Stan's death. In the name of progress, the town's main shopping thoroughfare, Saville Street, was ripped apart to make way for the car park of a new shopping center. A similar fate befell the second biggest thoroughfare, Bedford Street, when much of it and the land immediately behind it were cleared to make way for the shopping center itself. These scratched and faded black-and-white photos may not do justice to the original streets but still show that they were markedly superior to those that bear the same names today.

As a product of a middle-class and comparatively well-off family, Stan

Prudhoe Street, North Shields. 6881

The view east from outside North Shields' Theatre Royal towards Saville Street, the town's main shopping thoroughfare. Note the horse and cart to the right of the electric tram. (Courtesy of North Tyneside Local Studies Library.)

Top: The view east from Borough Bank along Saville Street. Note, in the middle of the image, the Central Palace of Varieties portico and the name of the theater painted high on the western wall of the building. *Above:* The view east from outside the Primitive Methodist Church on Saville Street (on the site occupied by Woolworth's until 2009).(Courtesy of North Tyneside Local Studies Library.)

Top: The view east from the junction of Camden Street with Saville Street showing the Town Hall in the middle of the image. *Above:* The view east along Charlotte Street from outside the Town Hall, showing Lambert's Commercial School and Post Office to the left and the Albion Assembly Rooms to the right. (Courtesy of North Tyneside Local Studies Library.)

had a private education that was markedly different from that of most other boys of his own age in North Shields who would have been attending schools paid for mainly out of the public purse.[1] However, if the pompous and ill-tempered portrayal of teachers in Laurel and Hardy's films is based on the impressions Stan had of his own teachers, it would seem that it was not necessarily money well spent. His education began in the basement of 34 Dockwray Square in a small establishment run by Miss R. Mason. Subsequently, he went for a time to a school in Tynemouth called, rather grandly, Jesmond College. Stan himself refers to it only as "Gordon's" because it was a small affair run by James Gordon. Although Stan did not hold him in high regard, Gordon was sufficiently distinguished to hold a B.A. degree and be a Fellow of the Royal Society of Arts at a time when very few people enjoyed access to higher education. He appears to have used the name Jesmond College for his little academy because he had previously run a similar school in Newcastle.[2] By 1901, James was living at 2 Newcastle Terrace, Tynemouth. Stan's own unfavorable account of the school is entirely consistent with this one-man setup:

> He was quite a character, he collected Cats, do'nt think he ever let them out of the house — you could smell the joint from Jarrow, the fish quay was like a garden of roses compared. The old screwball used to write poetry & we had to sit and listen to it all day long, his favourite one was "Ode to the Tyneside"— used to add new verses to it every day & ask our opinion. I once told him I did'nt like it & had to stand in the corner for an hour.[3]

Stan went on to explain that, after this episode, he was sent to what he "believed" was Tynemouth College. The most obvious candidate for that school is what is currently known as King's School. Unfortunately, there is no documentary evidence that Stan attended it. In response to my request for information, the current Alumni Development Officer explained that records for the school at that period are very sketchy and that at some stage the form lists had been destroyed. However, given that Tynemouth College was just around the corner from Gordon's Jesmond College, what is now King's School remains by far the most likely of the possibilities; some older former pupils claimed to have recalled seeing Stan's name on the now discarded school record boards. In a letter to the Local Studies Library in North Shields in 1997, A.S. Angus wrote: "My father and his brother Kenneth both attended what was then known as

Tynemouth School ... and it was Kenneth who told me quite definitely that he had been in the same class as Stan Laurel."[4]

Surprisingly, given that Tynemouth was only a mile away from his home in Dockwray Square, Stan went to school in Tynemouth as a boarder. The reason for that, he suggested in a letter in 1955, was that he was always in "trouble at home."

In 1963, Stan told one of his correspondents that he was also given piano and violin lessons. He did not volunteer how long they had lasted or how well he had done. All he confided was: "No, I never played any instrument during my career — I took lessons as a kid — Piano — Violin, but I just was'nt the type for a musical career.!" (Notice Stan's punctuation.) He may have been unduly modest about his musical prowess. We know that he owned a grand piano which he played to entertain his family and friends, and a photograph exists showing him playing a duet with Roach Studio's musical director Marvin Hatley (Skretvedt, 1987, p. 337). There is also no doubt that he could hold a tune. Although it is his partner Oliver who is renowned for his fine, trained singing voice, Stan made a genuine musical contribution to their *Blue Ridge Mountains of Virginia* recording, which when reissued posthumously in 1975 reached second in the UK hit singles chart and remained in the Top Ten for ten weeks.

Stan's time in North Shields was limited after the age of 12 because, from the start of January 1902, he was sent as a boarder to the King James I Grammar School in Bishop Auckland. That arrangement lasted for only six months when, convinced that Stan was not learning enough because the regime was too lenient, his father sent him elsewhere. Stan's own account of his short time at the school indicates that his father's action was understandable — especially given that he was probably paying handsomely for the privilege of this private grammar school education:

> I can remember just as clearly as yesterday when I was at school in Bishop Auckland.... It was a boarding school and, after the kids had gone to bed, Bates would come and take me into his private study where he and a couple of other masters were relaxing with a bottle. Bates would then have me entertain them with jokes, imitations, what-the-hell have you — anything for a laugh. I must have been awful but they seemed to get a big kick out of it, and I played many return engagements there.... I don't think playing to Bates and the other masters helped my education any as I was given a lot of privileges and a lot of my backwardness in class was overlooked —

which many times since I've regretted.... Once in a while I wonder what would have happened if I had been a good student [Stan Laurel quoted by McCabe, 2004, p. 8].

If the standard of the grammar and punctuation in Stan's letters in later life are indicative of how well he attended to his lessons at school, then Stan's father had good reason for concern at his son's lack of academic progress. Stan himself was proud to boast in a letter in 1958, "I think I have the honour of [having] been the worst scholar that ever attended there!" He was taken away from his easy life in Bishop Auckland and packed off to the Gainford Academy about ten miles away, to the west of Darlington. There he joined about 80 other boarders at a school which had been set up in 1818 by the Congregational Minister, the Reverend William Bowman. One can only assume it had a reputation for more strict discipline than the St. James I Grammar School in Bishop Auckland.[5]

In later life, Stan admitted to a correspondent that he had felt lonely in his spells away from home at boarding school and also that his being away and his family's theatrical background meant that they were rarely all at home together:

FEB.15th.1962.

My Dear ...

So sorry my taking so long to acknowledge your Xmas Day letter, I've intended to do so several times but I guess I've got that Manana complex — have so much unanswered mail, am really ashamed. Anyway, rest assured Betty, I am not offended — your letter in fact was most interesting reminiscing & describing your lonely Xmas days in boarding school when you were a little girl — it was really touching — having experienced that boarding school routine myself as a kid I know just how lonesome you felt — I spent most of my early days in boarding school due to my folks being theatrical — I can only remember two or three times the Family being altogether at home & then for very short periods. ...

Trust alls well & happy.

Bye dear — God Bless.

As ever:

Perhaps inevitably, given his background, much of the time that Stan did spend in North Shields was given over to things with a theatrical flavor. The earliest documented evidence that we have of him taking part in a theatrical performance was in 1897. Thanks to seven small photographs that have been passed down from Stan's father to his daughter Beatrice and, in due course, her family; we know that at least three of the Jefferson children performed a play in the backyard of their house called *The Rivals of Dockwray Square*. It is obvious that it was not a simple impromptu affair and serious thought had gone into the production. The bare brick walls and the yard's uneven paving stones may have been their stage but obvious efforts had been made to make it look more convincing. Attached to the wall about 6 feet (2m) from the ground was a length of wood about 6 feet (2m) long. From it hung a painted backcloth (weighted down with another length of wood). The backcloth lent perspective to the scene, with a foreground of trees and bushes which led the eye to a landscape beyond. On the "stage," at the foot of the backdrop, was a white rug which the photos show was turned in different directions for different scenes in the play. Completing the stage furniture was a tall potted plant which, like the rug, occupied different positions depending on the scene.

The photos suggest a cast list of only three: Stan, his older brother Gordon and his younger sister Beatrice. Although some effort may have gone into the staging of the play, the players were not in costume. The children appear to be wearing their Sunday best. Beatrice is in a pretty dress. Both boys are wearing knickerbockers, waistcoats with watches and chains, and jackets with flowers in their button holes. Gordon's outfit is topped off with an Eton collar: Stan's is a larger, floppier affair.

We do not know whether the play was penned for the children by their mother or father or whether it was a creation of one or more of the children. There is certainly no firm evidence that the play had been written by Stan, which some newspapers claimed was the case when the photos were first made public. What little we know about the plot comes from the photos themselves and the block-capital handwritten notes on their reverse, which were probably written by Beatrice in later years.

The play was simple in conception: two young men were rivals for the affections of the beautiful young Ran Ran played by Beatrice Olga. Her suitors were Ratty played by Gordon and Stupie played by Stan — suggesting that Stan may have become type-cast at an unusually early age! Beatrice's notes explain how she opted initially for Stupie: "Being stupid I picked Stupie!" The notes then explain that Ratty was not prepared to take her decision lying down. "Ratty being stupid too decides to settle her choice once and for all. May the best man win!" Jackets were then removed and pistols drawn. As the rival suitors stood back to back, examining their weapons before taking up their dueling positions, Ran Ran was heard to shout from off stage, "No! No! Not that!" At this point in the play, Ran Ran rushed back on to center stage and, according to the notes, tripped over the rug and brought down the scenery. Alas it is not clear if Beatrice is merely recording an unfortunate, unintended accident or whether this was a planned part of the comic melodrama! What her notes do tell us is that they all recovered and continued with "the blood curdling scene until Ran Ran intervened, took hold of the combatants raised ready-to-shoot arms and announced an ingenious if not entirely legal solution to the dispute. "Stop! I'll marry you both." The rival suitors agreed that "half a loaf was better than no loaf at all" and shook hands. In the final scene, after they had donned their jackets again, they settled down to what the audience must have been expected to believe was a happy (albeit bigamous) marriage. Beatrice records on the reverse of the seventh and final photo, "All's well that ends well. Ran Ran bakes an apple pie to celebrate." The final photo shows Ran Ran seated demurely on a chair, with Ratty and Stupie reclining on the mat at her feet, with cups of tea to suggest a scene of now domestic bliss!

The presence of the wooden rail secured to the backyard wall to hold the backcloth suggests that comparable productions may have taken place on other occasions. What we do know is that Stan, whether or not in conjunction with his brothers and sisters, used his Dockwray Square backyard as a place to entertain his friends. In 1958 he received a letter from a 14 year old Gary Arnold who had set up his own Laurel and Hardy Club and had written to Stan for ideas on what activities they might do in the Club. Stan replied:

> ... why do'nt you try amateur theatricals, am sure there must be some talent among your members for acting, singing and dancing. You could put on little shows. You would have a lot of fun doing short plays & dressing up in costume & putting on make-up — you could copy some of the TV shows and also do ideas of your own. That would give you all plenty to do. I used to do this when I was a kid & got a lot of enjoyment out of it. It was really interesting. In the summer time I put on shows in the back yard for friends and neighbors & had a wonderful time entertaining them ... [see Stan Laurel's letter dated 3 March 1958 at http://www.StanLaurelLetters.com/letters.htm].

4. Boyhood Years

Not all Stan's experience of playing to audiences was limited to the backyard of his home in Dockwray Square. We know that he had a foretaste of what was to come in terms of playing to a large audience when he was just nine years old in 1900.

During the Boer Wars in South Africa, the relief of the seven-month siege of the small town of Mafeking was celebrated throughout Britain with morale-boosting hype out of all proportion to its strategic significance. To convey some impression of the kind of world in which the young Stanley Jefferson was growing up, just a little of the coverage given to the relief of Mafeking in the local Shields newspaper of the time is set out below.[6] The following are examples of the many headlines, relating to every possible aspect of the story, which appeared in the *Shields Daily News* of May 19, 1901. *The Shields Daily News* was a serious newspaper, it should be added, much more comparable in style and coverage to the revered *Times* of the period than the tabloid style and focus of today's local English newspapers.

> THE RELIEF OF MAFEKING
> BOERS ABANDON SIEGE
> UNPARALLELED SCENES IN LONDON AND WINDSOR
> SURGING MASSES CROWDING THE STREETS
> PATRIOTISM AND ENTHUSIASM EVERYWHERE
> HOW THE BRITISH FLAG WAS KEPT FLYING

This is how the newspaper described the immediate local reaction:

The scene at North Shields on the receipt of the news of the relief of Mafeking shortly after ten o'clock was of the most enthusiastic description. It was first notified by the explosion of fourteen gun cotton charges.... The previous night's experience made very many people sceptical of the truth of the statement. Still this did not prevent thousands from leaving their homes and rushing wildly in search of information.... It was not long before confirmation came. It was followed by an outburst of intense excitement and jubilation. The principal streets of the town quickly became densely thronged.... Innumerable processions were formed, and the streets were paraded until early morning.

Accompanying all the accounts of the relief of Mafeking itself and the international, national and local reactions to it was a jingoistic poem. It is inconceivable that such a poem would be published in any British newspaper today. Just three of the nine strident and jubilant verses are quoted below.

> Flash, flash it forth to all the world,
> And let your banners be unfurl'd
> Mafeking is free!
> Tingles the blood of high and low
> For right and might our cheeks to glow
> Mafeking is free!
> To Mother Queen will joy impart
> Soothing her woman's anxious heart
> Mafeking is free!

Arthur Jefferson, the local showman, was prominent in making the arrangement for the pageant and parade that followed. He received a public acknowledgment of his contribution in later years and it is unlikely to be a coincidence that the starting point for the parade was his own Dockwray Square. We know from the *Shields Daily News* of May 21, 1900, that on Saturday, May 19, 1900, work was suspended; Union Jacks unfurled; red, white and blue bunting was strung between shops and houses; and that people lined the streets waiting for the pageant and parade to pass by. Although only the paragraph in italics below contains a specific reference to the young Stanley Jefferson, a little more has been included because it gives an indication of how excited he must have been by his role at the heart of such a major event and the public's reaction to what was probably his first dramatic appearance in public:

An early start was made. Several charges of gun cotton were exploded in the forenoon from the river frontage, these being followed by welcome screams of the sirens of steamers on the river.... Excepting for the occasional exploding of bombs, repeated outbursts of sirens on the river, and informal processions of youngsters got up in true military style, there was nothing more until 3 o'clock, when the band of the *Wellesley* ... and the whole ship's company under arms came ashore and paraded in Dockwray Square.... In the presence of a large concourse of persons they left the Square and marched through the principal streets of the town.[7] They were joined by the Work-house children and band, and Haley's Prize Choir ... Patriotic songs were played and sung during the march, and the route of the procession was densely thronged with people.

A conspicuous feature was seen at the head of the procession. Master Roland Park, attired in full regimentals representing Lord Roberts, and mounted on a pony, was the central figure. He was attended by a perfect little picture which excited much comment as Masters Jefferson, Walton and Davidson, attired in the uniform of the Imperial Yeomanry, made among the spectators.

At night, however, the principal events took place. All householders had been requested to illuminate their houses, and the response was really remarkable, and showed the extent of loyalty and patriotism in the borough.... The chief attraction was in Northumberland Square [and, as this was the home of his friend Roland Park, Stan was likely to have been party to everything that was going on]. Every house was illuminated. There had been keen competition, the residents had vied with each other in the endeavour to make a grand and unequalled show and the effect was splendid. Wonderland was not in it. In addition to the illumination there, the band of the Sub-Marine Miners ... occupied the area and discoursed pleasing and appropriate music, while in the north-west corner, lime-light views connected with the war were displayed upon a sheet for the delectation of the thousands of persons who were gathered to see them and the other attractions. The square outside the area was densely packed with people and the utmost good order and good feeling prevailed [*Shields Daily News*, May 21, 1900].[8]

Much more is known about Stan's early theatrical pretensions thanks to an unpublished biography by his father, which John McCabe discovered while looking through Stan's papers after his death. The biography, entitled *Turning the Pages*, seems to have been completed in 1939. Although Arthur Jefferson was anxious to see it in print, Stan thwarted his father's plans. The reasons he offered later were that he disliked its "florid Victorian style" and felt it was "interspersed with windy disquisitions on irrelevant matters." Readers can judge for themselves whether or not his father had a florid Victorian style from the extract below but, fortunately for us, McCabe realized that there was valuable material in the book and considered it sufficiently important to quote from at length in his own 1974 book, *The Comedy World of Stan Laurel*. The quotations included below provide us with some fascinating insights into the world of the young Stanley Jefferson and a foretaste of the kind of comic situations he was later to be creating for cinema audiences throughout the world. It seems that Stan spent all his pocket money on things related to the world of entertainment, such as toy theaters, marionettes and shadow-graphs (actors posing in silhouette behind illuminated screens). But, far from satisfying him, they seem to have made him ambitious for something more substantial. He wanted his own theater.

... Stan begged me to convert the attic of our home in North Shields [in Ayton House] into a miniature theater ... I agreed, calling upon my local theater staff to carry out the work ... producing ... with seating for about 20 to 30 people ... a perfect replica of the average small theater of that period. Stan, assisted by several "dying to act" boys and girls was hard at work inaugurating the "Stanley Jefferson Amateur Dramatic Society" — featuring said S.J. as Director, Manager, Stage Manager, Author, Producer, and Leading Man."

Stan must have been about 12 at the time.[9] He made use of the theater by writing for himself a series of roles which combined both heroism and comedy. It also seems that Stan had acquired something of his father's business acumen because he charged for participation as well as admission. Stan was flexible when it came to payment. If children were short of ready cash, he was prepared to barter and accept payment in kind, especially if the items could prove useful as theatrical props. Harold, the boy whom Stan wanted to play the villain in his final play, had nothing to offer except two white mice. Stan readily accepted them as payment because he judged that Harold had ideal facial features for the part.

Stan's script was not highly original but it showed that he had already developed an appreciation of the kind of theatrical action and dialog that his audience would expect and appreciate. His father is a little dismissive, describing it as a flagrant piece of composite plagiarism, made up of different elements that Stan had seen at his theaters over the years. But that in itself can be cited as evidence of how theatrically astute Stan had become even at that tender age. He had obviously not just been entertained by the performances he had seen. He had observed what it was that made audiences respond positively and then tried to replicate them in his own material.

After the rehearsals; the distribution of publicity notices to drum up an audience and the sale of tickets, the evening of the performance arrived with every seat taken in the little theater. The performance began quietly — literally. The overture consisted of a music box playing *The Blue Bells of Scotland* which could not be heard beyond the front row. But,

Opposite: Stan Jefferson, age 9, standing with his hand on the horse's bridle, prior to the North Shields Relief of Mafeking celebrations on May 19, 1900. The boy on the horse is unidentified. (Courtesy of Huntley Jefferson Woods [Stan Laurel's nephew].)

when the curtain rose, each performer received loud applause "depending largely upon the numerical strength of the parental cliques involved." The fact that Stan did especially well, his father suspected, was probably due to the fact that he was sometimes able to distribute free passes to the Theatre Royal. Arthur wrote:

> The first act, ending with Stan's oath to "track the monster to his lair," evoked tumultuous applause and quivering excitement. The second act during which Stan true to his oath "cornered his prey" called upon that monster to surrender ... [and] ended in a life or death struggle, rousing the audience to a high pitch of excitement, the parents taking sides with their respective offspring, and the juvenile females with the boy they favoured most. The audience egged the actors on with cries of "Stick it, Stan!" or "Good lad, Harold!" ... Stan and Harold threw missiles, anything handy, at each other; then they cast off their outer garments in the struggle; clinched several times followed by a joint fall, and then came the stereotyped rolling and rolling over the stage, backwards, then forwards!

Arthur Jefferson went on to explain that in the good old days no struggle was acclaimed by the audience unless accompanied by such antics and that the number of rolls determined the length of the applause. It seems, however, that by this stage in the performance the young Stanley and his co-performer Harold had somewhat lost the plot and their struggle had become just a little personal. As a result there was an unexpected climax to the fight. Stan and Harold thrashed about so much that they knocked over one of the paraffin oil lamps which served as a footlight. Within seconds, the flimsy side curtains were ablaze. By the time Arthur Jefferson returned with an extinguisher, the fire had spread to the wooden framework of the little theater that he had so lovingly created for Stan. Arthur continued:

> Genuine troupers both, the boys had continued their mighty struggle all the way through the fire, and were totally oblivious to the flames which were surrounding them! They persevered in their fight until pulled apart by their respective mothers.... My doctor was called and outside of singed eyebrows, Harold was fine, and was forthwith despatched by cab to his home. But poor old Stan! He had suffered more than a few burns. His grief at the play's ending was truly tragic.

That was not the end of the matter. Foreshadowing the tit-for-tat action-reaction momentum that was to characterize so many Laurel and

Hardy films, Stan's friend Harold demanded satisfaction. He wrote to Stan, blaming him for the loss of his eyebrows and demanded the return of his "in-lieu of money" contribution to the evening's proceedings — namely his two mice. Whereas Stan's later screen persona would have reacted without thinking and escalated the conflict, the real Stan had the wit to ask for his father's advice before responding. He was reminded of the old adage that "a soft answer turneth away wrath" and advised to write a diplomatic letter in reply. His father also had the good sense to suggest that Stan let him see the reply before posting it. Stan's initial draft went like this:

Ayton House
North Shields

Dear Harold:

I think it is very unkind of you to write me like this.

The fire was all your fault; if you had let go of my throat when you saw my face going all red, we shouldn't have rolled over as far as the lamps. You have lost nothing over the accident. I have lost my theater. Dad is having it all done away with for good and all — and all my pocket money since it started. I am sorry about your eyebrows being burned off, of course, but they will grow again. And don't forget that I got some nasty burns too as well as being nearly strangled to death by you.

You once told me that the men in your father's slaughterhouse had once let you help them to kill a pig. I didn't believe you then but I do now. In fact, after the way you tried to kill me, I should believe you now if you told me that you had killed a cow all by yourself.

Stanley

Surprisingly, given that Arthur had urged Stanley to write a diplomatic response, it seems that he only insisted that Stan rewrite the final sentence of the letter. So, instead of maintaining that "after the way you tried to kill me, I should believe you now if you told me that you had killed a cow all by yourself," Stan added:

I cannot agree to returning your two white mice but I'll tell you what I will do. If they get married and have babies, I will divide them with you. If you want to be friends I do, if you don't, I don't.

Stanley

Those of you who don't like stories without "proper" endings will be disappointed to learn that Stan's father did not record if the white mice ever did "cohabit profitably" or if Stan ever returned them to Harold.

Laurel with his mother at the gate of what is believed to be Ayton House, his second North Shields home. (Courtesy of Lois Laurel-Hawes [Stan Laurel's daughter].)

Although we have a detailed account of only this single production in Stan's little theatre in Ayton House, we do know there were others — although he may not have always played to capacity audiences. During his visit to the UK in 1932, an old childhood friend, Lena, who had been unable to get to see him, gave Stan's father a letter to pass on to him. Among other things, the letter contained a reference to an occasion when Lena was the only member of the audience in Stan's little theatre. In his hand-written, three page reply, Stan recalled all the happy times they had enjoyed together as children and added, "I got a big laugh out of you telling me about you being my only audience at my little Theatre — you must have been bored to death."

We know that Stan tried his hand at almost anything he could that related to the world of entertainment. His father described how he spent much of his pocket money on such things as toy theatres, marionettes and shadow-graphs and we know from Stan's own 1958 letter to Gary Arnold that he enjoyed dressing up, putting on make-up and performing in shows and short plays for the entertainment of his friends and neighbors. According to Stan, he also had a lot of fun playing with a toy phonograph. In the 1932 letter to his childhood friend Lena he recalled how her brother Percy had bought him a toy phonograph. But Stan had not been satisfied simply to listen to whatever was already recorded for that machine. What he wrote to Lena was, "Do you remember when Percy bought me a Toy Phonograph & we made our own records on it. Just seems like yesterday it's so clear to me." From a tender age Stan was determined not only to entertain but to involve himself in the production of entertainment: a determination that was to serve him so well in later life.

5

From Theatrical Obscurity
to Film Stardom

Arthur Jefferson left North Shields with his family in 1905 and they made their home in Glasgow. It is not entirely clear why the family moved. In one account, Arthur explained that they left North Shields because he had to give the lease of the Glasgow Metropole his personal attention but, in another, suggested that they had moved primarily because of his wife Madge's ill health. Unfortunately, the move did not help to restore it and Madge died in 1908 at age 47.[1]

The Jeffersons moved first to Buchanan Drive in the suburb of Rutherglen and then to Stonelaw Road, just around the corner. The move to Scotland meant two more changes in schooling for Stan. He first attended Stonelaw High School (sometimes known as Rutherglen Academy) but soon moved to Queen's Park Secondary School. His attendance record was far from perfect and he frequently played truant. One of his hideaways was an old shed where he became part of an entertainment troupe run by a friend, Willy Walker.

Stan explained to John McCabe that eventually his father accepted the situation, allowing Stan to leave school and start work in the Metropole, adding up the proceeds of the gallery box office each night. That did not give Stan any satisfaction but having a genuine reason for being on the premises, and lots of opportunities to go backstage to talk to the performers, suited him very much more than being at school. His father assumed, or at least hoped, that in time Stan would realize that, however much pleasure could be derived from performing, writing or directing, a sound financial future lay in being the man in charge. But, far from dampening Stan's enthusiasm, his contact with the Metropole's performers merely whetted his appetite for more. Stan was determined to be on the stage and not behind it or in front of it.

5. From Theatrical Obscurity to Film Stardom

His opportunity to try his hand on the stage was made easier by the nearby presence of the Britannia Theatre of Varieties and Panopticon. It was very much more than a theater. It was at one and the same time a place where for a half-penny one could use the gramophone (a technological wonder in its day); turn the handle of a penny-winder to see what the butler had seen (in effect a mini-personal cinema); view the exhibits in the sideshows and museum or watch the acts in the theater. Stan spent several weeks building up an act based, he readily admitted, on heavily plagiarized material and, unbeknownst to his father, tried it out first at the amateur night at the Britannia. What he could not have anticipated was that his father would choose the night of his next appearance to walk round for a chat with his friend Albert Pickard, the Britannia manager.[2] Albert, assuming Arthur knew that Stan was about to appear, greeted him with: "You're just in time. Stan is due on in about five minutes" (McCabe, 2004, p. 10).

> When he again sneaked out to go to the Britannia, Stan was keener than ever to avoid being caught by his father, for in a parcel under his arm was a pair of his father's check trousers, cut down to fit Stan; a long frock coat, also A.J.'s; the cover off his father's umbrella, which had been fastened to a cane to make a comic gamp; and a stick of red grease paint. The latter was for painting Stan's nose red, of which he said, "You couldn't be funny in those days, unless you had a red nose" [Marriot, 1993, p. 17].

Stan appears to have received a good round of applause from the audience but not a little of it was caused indirectly by the intimidating presence of his father. Realizing that Arthur would recognize the hat, frock coat and cut-down check trousers as his own, Stan left the stage in something of a hurry. In his unpublished biography of Stan, Arthur Jefferson described what happened when Stan spotted him:

> Giving a subdued yell of horrified astonishment, [Stan] dropped my topper which thereupon rolled toward the footlights. Stan pursued it, tried to grab it and in so doing kicked it accidentally into the orchestra where one of the musicians made a rush to retrieve it and stepped on it, squashing it thoroughly! Then Stan made a dash for the exit but his luck was out. As he ran off, he came in contact with a steel hook fixed in the wings for a trapeze act and the hook ripped off half the skirt of my beautiful frock coat. Exit ... loud applause! My music hall friend was greatly pleased with the act. He said that the "business" of smashing the topper and the tearing of the coat was extremely funny! Groaning inwardly, I departed for the Met, feeling

certain that Stan, who was always a very plucky kid, would return and face the music. He did — very forlorn, very apprehensive of the reception that he would get from me. Imagine his astonishment and joy when I received him with open arms and congratulations and promises to help him achieve his ambition [McCabe, 2004, pp. 11–12].

Stan described that fateful meeting in the following words:

I removed my makeup and rushed back to the Met' to hide from my father's wrath, but he was already there. He called me into his office where, for what seemed like several minutes, neither of us spoke. Finally, he glanced up at me and said, "Not bad son but where on earth did you get all those gags?" Fearfully, I told him the whole story and waited for the storm to burst. Slowly, he rose to his feet, "Have a whisky-and-soda?" he asked quite casually. At first I could not believe my ears, but when it dawned upon me I seemed to grow six inches in as many seconds. My boyhood was behind me — Dad was accepting me as a man! Then I did the silliest thing — I burst out crying.... Putting his arm around me he led me into the theater bar and, with eyes glistening, introduced me to his friends as "My son, Stan — the new comedian." Was I proud? I still think it was the greatest moment of my life [Stan Laurel quoted by Marriot, 1993, pp. 18–20].[3]

Stan's Theatrical Apprenticeship

Despite the praise, Stan's father must have had reservations about his son trying his luck as a stand-up comedian in the music halls of early 20th century Britain. Legitimate drama (even in the mold of Jefferson's melo-drama) had a long, respectable history and was socially acceptable but music hall, with its more recent London origins, was a different matter. It was frowned upon by the establishment of the day not least because most of the venues were little more than bars and taverns where the audience continued to consume alcohol throughout the entertainment. It was only after the first Royal Variety Command Performance in 1912, when the acts appeared before King George V, that this type of popular entertainment received the establishment's stamp of approval.[4]

To help Stan on his way, his father used his influence to get him a place in the Levy and Cardwell Juvenile Pantomime Company. For the benefit of readers not from the UK, a pantomime is a still popular form of distinctive "tongue-in-cheek" musical comedy performed in the winter months. Based on a children's story or nursery rhyme, it is aimed primarily at children and involves considerable audience participation. In a set of biographical notes which Stan produced in 1932 for the publicity department of the Roach Studio, he described the Levy and Cardwell Juvenile shows as similar to the satirical and clean burlesque shows of the U.S., but with the performers ranging in age from 6 to 18. In the first season in 1907 he played a minor part in *The Sleeping Beauty* alongside 12-year-old George Wood, the headlined star of the show, who came from Jarrow, just across the river from North Shields. Wee Georgie Wood (only 4'9" when fully grown) went on to become a well-known variety artist in the UK and he and Stan remained friends.[5]

The accounts by John McCabe and A.J. Marriot about what Stan did after his first pantomime season differ in their detail. However, the strong supporting evidence provided by Marriot makes his the more convincing (McCabe, 2004, p. 12, and Marriot, 1993, p. 22). Stan played the stable boy in *The Gentleman Jockey*, produced by the Edward Marris musical comedy company. He then enjoyed a brief spell in the *Home from the Honeymoon* sketch, towards the end of its run in the prestigious Moss Empire theaters. What Stan did not explain in his 1932 biographical note is that he had co-authored the sketch. Fortunately, Marriot's diligent research uncovered that it and four other sketches had been written by A.J. Jefferson *and* Son and were advertised as such in the trade paper *The Stage* in 1908.[6]

Just days before the first night of the 1908 pantomime season, Stan's mother died and he had his first bitter taste of the theater's credo "The show must go on."[7] Once again Stan had only a minor role in the pantomime (*The House That Jack Built*) but attracted favorable mentions from the press as he had done in the previous season. It seems to have been after this run that he had another stint with the Marris Company, in a comedy role in the melodrama *Alone in the World*. From then on, he tried to go it alone and make a living as a stand-up comedian. He was billed as "Young Stanley Jefferson — He of the Funny Ways." He readily admitted that he did not have a distinctive act of his own at this early stage in his career and copied freely from the acts of more established comedians. He could get away with it, he explained, because (in a world still without mass communications such as radio, film and TV) the established music hall stars would never appear in the second-rate venues in which he was appearing.

Stan may have loved being in front of the footlights, but life on the road was not much fun. He was still a teenager, earning very little, and living apart from his family at a time when it was still usual for young people to remain at home with their parents until (and often after) marriage; there must have been many lonely nights when he regretted following his dream. Although he was able to see the amusing side of those early experiences when relating them as a successful Stan Laurel, they must have been most disheartening to the still *un*successful Stan Jefferson. Sharing a bedroom in a theatrical lodging house with three fat men and a performing seal, and then having to pay extra for the privilege of sharing with one man and his six trick cycles, might make good material for a humorous story. But, for a teenager who had just lost his mother, and had no idea whether or not he was going to be able to make a success of his chosen occupation, such experiences must have encouraged serious bouts of self-doubt.

Stan decided that he needed more experience as an actor and briefly joined the Percy Williams Company. The first play in which he appeared folded after just a few weeks and the manager ran off with the takings. Ironically, had the play been a runaway success, the world might never have known the great Stan Laurel. Fortunately for him and for us, this still gauche, unemployed 19-year-old youth turned up at the Grand Theatre in Glasgow for an interview with the celebrated impresario Fred Karno. In one account, Stan gave the impression that he turned up uninvited; in another he suggested that he had been "scouted" by Karno; and in a third he implied that his father had arranged the meeting for him. The crucial fact, however, is undisputed. He left with a place in the Fred Karno Company of Comedians and joined, amongst many others, the already established star Charlie Chaplin. A new phase in his career had begun.

Karno and America

In April 1910, during rehearsals for the Karno Company's *Jimmy the Fearless,* when Chaplin declined the leading role, Stan took his place and was thrust into the limelight. For a week, Stan played to enthusiastic houses and had the wonderful experience of taking curtain calls. At that point, Chaplin decided he would like to play the role of Jimmy after all.

Inevitably, there has been speculation that this was because the star felt threatened by the reception Stan was receiving. But whatever the reason, it meant that Stan's fleeting glimpse of glory was gone and he returned to his initial role as just another one of the boys.[8]

Soon after the end of a long run, Karno had further good news for Stan. He had been selected to go on a tour of the United States. Alas the tour neither started nor ended well for Stan. The Company did not travel in the style they had anticipated. They appear to have missed the liner on which they were originally booked and were obliged to travel instead in a converted cattle-boat. During the rough 11 days at sea, many of the cast members were seasick, which made rehearsing difficult. Arriving three days late in Montreal and only one day before they were due to open in New York, required them to make a hurried train ride to their destination. Whether because of this limited time for rehearsals, or the inherent nature of the show, it was panned by the critics. The Company dropped it in favor of *Mumming Birds,* an already established Karno favorite which, in different guises, ran off and on for an unbelievable 45 years (Marriot, 1993, pp. 27, 31). That proved more successful and the planned six-week tour was extended.

Stan knew he was gaining valuable experience, but was unhappy with the low wage he was paid by Karno. He earned $20 a week (about £4 at the then exchange rate). Out of this he was expected to pay his own rail fares, hotel bills and food. As Stan pointed out, "Even though everything was cheap at that time, $20 wasn't enough to travel on and take care of yourself, so it ended up with three or four of us sharing a room" (Owen-Pawson and Mouland, 1984, p. 104). When Stan and a few others asked for a raise they were refused. So Stan and another member of the troupe, Arthur Dandoe, resigned and returned to England on the *Lusitania*—in steerage class.[9]

Stan and Arthur worked together and had some success in the English music halls before going their separate ways. After the split, Stan was in and out of out of regular work for a year. He had to ask his brother Gordon for help. He also shared his London flat and did odd jobs, including typing scripts, before a chance meeting with an old friend resulted in a return trip to the U.S. in 1912 with a new Karno Company — on improved pay. He again worked (and lived) closely with Charlie Chaplin. When Charlie began to receive rave reviews, he was lured away from the Karno Company to make pictures for Mack Sennett, soon to become known as the King of Comedy. With its star gone, the tour folded. The Karno Company returned to the UK but Stan decided to stay on in the U.S. and try his hand at vaudeville.[10]

Although Stan may have spent only a short time with the Karno Company, he learned a great deal from it. Karno's view of comedy had a lasting influence on his later screen persona and also that of Chaplin. As Stan told Arthur Friedman in 1957, "We all had the same fundamental groundwork: Karnoism." Karno believed that comedians were at their most effective when doleful and able to wring sympathy as well as laughter from an audience. He also favored a heavy reliance on body language to complement comic situations with only limited dialog to heighten the visual aspect of the comedy. Stan's Karno experience stood him in good stead when he began to make films. When he was making silent films, the lack of dialog in no way inhibited him. When the talkies arrived, he already had a pattern to follow. He did not create situations in which the dialog was dominant. From the experience he had enjoyed with Karno, he knew that limited dialog would enhance his essentially visual comedy. It was, of course, that essentially visual nature of Laurel and Hardy's comedy that was to make it so readily accessible to audiences all over the world.

Vaudeville and Cinema

On the previous tour Stan returned to the UK early. This time he stayed on in the United States. He toured first with the Karno comics Edgar and Wren Hurley (initially as the Three Comiques but subsequently Hurley, Stan and Wren and then the Keystone Trio), with Stan playing a character modeled on Chaplin. Then, about 1915, he joined Alice and Baldwin Cooke and they toured as the Stan Jefferson Trio. After a comparatively successful few years, the act broke up when Stan met the Australian singer and dancer, Mae Charlotte Dahlberg in 1917. It was probably about then that Stan played a comic role in a magic act known as Martini and Maximillian for a short time while creating a new act for himself and Mae. Although they had a relationship that hindered rather than helped his career, she does appear to have suggested the change of name by which Stan would eventually become known throughout the world. We know from what Stan told Arthur Friedman in 1957 that he decided that a shorter name would be an advantage because it would take up less space on billboards and so mean that it could be in bigger letters. He also told John McCabe that he was conscious of the fact that Stan Jefferson was made up of 13 letters — a supposedly unlucky number — and he felt that his luck improved after he changed it (McCabe, 1976, p. 47). However, these remarks explain only why he chose to replace Jefferson, not why he opted for Laurel rather than some other shorter name. In his 1957 interview, in response to a direct question, Stan said he could not remember why he had opted for the name Laurel. He made a similar point to McCabe: "Funny — I don't know why I picked Laurel. Honestly can't remember. Just sounded good, I guess" (McCabe, 1976, p. 47).

It could be that Stan's memory lapse was diplomatic or Freudian in character because his former partner Mae later told McCabe that she suggested the name Laurel to Stan. She recalled that she was looking through a book that had been left behind in a theater dressing room by a member of a previous act. She came across a drawing of the Roman General Scipio Africanus Major and noticed that he was wearing a laurel wreath.

> I looked at that headpiece of laurel, and that word stayed with me. I said it aloud, "Laurel, Laurel, Stan Laurel." Stan looked up from what he was doing and he said, "What?" I said, "Laurel. Stan Laurel. How about that for a name?" He repeated it out loud too. "Sounds very good." "That's how he got his name. It was that simple" [Mae Dahlberg quoted by McCabe, 2004, pp. 24–26].

While touring with Mae, Stan had his first film break. The owner of the Hippodrome Theatre in Los Angeles saw Stan's potential and advanced the money to make the equivalent of a demonstration film called *Nuts in May* (sometimes called *Just Nuts*) in 1917. Although Stan did not rate it highly, it was good enough to secure him a one-year contract with Universal Studios. It has been suggested that the main problem with his Universal films was not the quality of Stan's own contributions but those of his stage partner Mae, whom he insisted should be in the cast. However, as Louvish notes, most of the films they made together are now lost and there is no hard evidence that she was actually in all of them. For whatever reason,

Stan's contract was not renewed. He returned to vaudeville, making only occasional trips back to the film studios: in 1918, for example, to make five undistinguished one-reel films for Hal Roach. It was in one of those films that he appeared on screen for the first time with Oliver Hardy. As Stan recalls:

> There was nothing about the picture or our own personal relationship to suggest that we might ever become partners. He and I were just two working comics, glad to have a job — any job [Stan Laurel quoted by McCabe, 2004, p. 30].

In those early years, it was Oliver Hardy who had regular film work. In fact, he had already been in an astonishing 270 films by the time that he and Stan became a team. During the same period when Oliver was hard at work in film studios, Stan spent his time alternating between brief stints with a number of film studios and longer spells back in vaudeville. McCabe's biography of Stan lists his 1918–1920 vaudeville engagements to illustrate just how widely Stan traveled in the USA and Canada during those years. After another short stint at the Roach Studio in 1923, he was back on the road again.

There is a widespread view that Stan's film prospects continued to be damaged by his relationship with Mae. Stan wanted her included in any contract (probably because she vehemently insisted on it) but any studios with an interest in Stan did not have a comparable interest in her. When Stan was so down on his luck that he had patches in his trousers and cardboard inside his shoes to cover up the holes in the soles, his director friend Perce Pembroke approached Jo Rock and asked him if he could help. Rock advanced Stan a substantial sum of money to tide him over and decided to take a chance on making a series of films with him — but on the strict condition that Mae would not be involved in any way. That condition was not easily met and it took more than one confrontation and ultimatum before Mae eventually yielded. With a significant financial incentive, she returned to Australia.

In that same year, on the strength of his growing reputation as a creator of comic situations and gags, Stan also signed up with the Hal Roach Studio as a writer and director — although he remained contracted to Rock as an actor. So, ironically, when Stan did begin to work on a regular basis at the Hal Roach Studio in May 1925 (shortly before his 35th birthday), it was behind rather than in front of the cameras. In his third film he directed none other than Oliver "Babe" Hardy, whose first Roach film under contract (he had made other Roach films before being given a regular contract) was released in the very same month that Stan joined the studio. Stan went on to write or direct another eight films with Babe before they were brought together on screen.

Laurel and Hardy at Roach

By an often recounted coincidence, it was when Stan was pressed to stand in for Oliver (who had scalded his arm) that he went back in front of the cameras. It was also about this time that Stan was released from his contract with Rock and so was now free to act as well as write and direct for the Roach Studios. Thereafter, Stan and Oliver played together in over a dozen films until "the potential of playing them *against* one another was spotted and exploited" (Marriot, 1993, p. 40). It was only then that they both developed the instantly recognizable screen personas that made them so successful. Despite their long association with the film world, neither had developed a distinctive screen character that belonged to them and them alone — something Chaplin had achieved and exploited so very effectively from the very beginnings of his screen career. Instead, they had each played a multitude of different characters whether on screen together or separately. It seems that Leo McCarey first conceived of Laurel and Hardy as a team but, according to Frank Butler, the head of the Roach scenario department, it was Stan who developed the basic idea behind the boys' characters: dumbness combined with invincible innocence and, he might have added, invincible optimism (Skretvedt, 1987, p. 63). Moreover, as I shall explain in detail in the next chapter, it was Stan above all who was primarily responsible for the writing and direction of all of the most successful Laurel and Hardy films.

Laurel and Hardy's most successful films were made in what might seem the most improbable period for laughter: the prolonged worldwide depression of the 1930s. While no one was able to escape its effects entirely, the burden of the Depression was carried disproportionately by unemployed and under-employed workers and their families, concentrated in particular areas and regions. Making their deprivation worse was the fact that they had to endure their poverty alongside continual reminders that other members of their society were still enjoying the good life. In many of Laurel and Hardy's films they played the role of the dispossessed: people without a job, an education or even a family. But, though there was pathos in their films, they never wallowed in it. They were eternal optimists. Their innocence, friendship and loyalty enabled them to survive all the calamities that befell them. Their films became enormously popular. As Gehring reminds us, Will Rogers once described them as Hollywood's "best team of comedians and the favorites with all us movie folks as well as the audiences," and the film historian Leonard Maltin maintained that while Chaplin may have "commanded more attention ... it's doubtful that anyone generated more laughter or more love than Laurel and Hardy" (quoted by Gehring, 2007, p. 152).

There does not seem to be a consensus about what was their first appearance together as Laurel and Hardy, in the familiar roles they played for the next quarter of a century. Some suggest that it was *The Second Hundred Years* in which they played escaped convicts in striped prison garb. Others prefer to cite *Hats Off* in which they donned their trademark hats, and still others *Putting Pants on Philip*. For Louvish, the pivotal point came in the 1927 film *Duck Soup* when "Laurel and Hardy leap forth, almost full made" (Louvish, 2001, p. 199). What is noteworthy about the film is that it is based on a sketch written by Stan and his father 22 years earlier. The film carries the credit "Story based on *Home from the Honeymoon* by Arthur. J. Jefferson." Louvish adds, "Stan wrote the script, delineated the characters, decided on the plot and the gags" (Louvish, 2001, p. 201). So, it must have given both father and son great satisfaction that it was this particular family vehicle that launched Stan Laurel into cinema history. By then Stan was 37 and Oliver Hardy 35. Both had served long solo apprenticeships but as a comedy duo they soon became sensationally successful international film stars, and even after their deaths were featured on the postage stamps of at least twelve nations.[11]

Part of their international success can be attributed to the painstaking way the Laurel and Hardy films were made initially for foreign audiences. In the era of silent films, intertitles were easily translated. A wholly different approach was required with sound films. Initially, the Roach Studio did not resort to the visually obvious dubbing which became commonplace elsewhere. Films for foreign markets were actually re-shot scene by scene, with the cast (when they could handle it) speaking in the appropriate foreign language, i.e., French, German, Italian and Spanish. The fact that Stan and Oliver spoke their own dialog in their foreign films does not mean that they were genuinely fluent in all four languages. Nevertheless, the fact that other actors were sometimes substituted in key roles does indicate that Stan and Oliver could cope better than others with the daunting task of speaking convincingly and with appropriate nuances in languages that were not their own. Once the English version of a film was completed, French, German, Italian and Spanish interpreters would translate the script and write it out phonetically — along with the original English. That, Stan explained, was important so that they could employ appropriate intonation.

> We'd set up the camera, and we'd do the French version of the first scene. After the first scene, we'd hold the camera, and we'd do the German scene. And each scene we did four times, before we moved the camera for each different change. But [the foreign audiences] understood us perfectly, and I think that's what made it so popular. So when we finally went over there, they were amazed that we couldn't speak their language [quoted by Skretvedt, 1987, p. 184].

Although this was a time-consuming and expensive process, Hal Roach judged that it was worthwhile not only in terms of enhancing the standing of Laurel and Hardy with foreign audiences but also in terms of making money. He later added that the prices they were able to charge for these foreign versions of the Laurel and Hardy films were "fantastic" and that a two-reeler short in a country like the Argentine would be accorded the same respect as a full-length feature film (Hal Roach quoted by Skretvedt, 1987, p. 185). Eventually, MGM, who distributed the Laurel and Hardy films, insisted that Roach dub them like the other studios because the Spanish-speaking countries were demanding non-dubbed versions of all MGM's films!

Because there is not a consensus on which film represented the start of their partnership, it is not possible to make a definitive statement about how many films Laurel *and* Hardy made together. Moreover, in addition to deciding when they first became the comedy duo Laurel and Hardy, as distinct from just appearing in films together, it is not obvious whether or not to include their cameo roles and other special appearances, such as their 1943 contribution to the war effort *The Tree in a Test Tube*.[12] However, most would agree that they made at least 100 films together: 34 silent shorts, 41 sound shorts and 25 full length sound feature films.

Unlike many other silent stars, Laurel and Hardy made the transition to sound with remarkable ease. Brought up in the Karno tradition, Stan knew the importance of the visual in humor and how much could be achieved with only limited dialog. But that is not to say that Laurel and Hardy did not exploit the opportunities offered by sound when it came along. As well as the famous Laurel whimpered cry and Oliver's catch-phrase "That's another nice mess you've gotten me into," Stan introduced more elaborate verbal material into the films. Perhaps the most easily recognized device is when Laurel made an apparently sensible suggestion to Hardy — but one which required clarification. A puzzled Hardy would then ask him to repeat it only to have Laurel start with the prelude "Well ..." and then go on to produce a meaningless mangling of his first effort. It has been suggested that this device was probably an adaptation of the longer nonsensical anecdotes told on stage by Stan's comic music hall hero Dan Leno. Whatever the inspiration, Stan's verbal nonsense was entirely consistent with his own screen persona and proved wonderfully effective.

Although Laurel and Hardy were often in costume in their mainstream films, they are remembered most of all for the familiar outfits they wore in so many of them: their ill-fitting suits and wing-collared shirts (the cuffs of which Stan tied with string); Stan's bow-tie and Ollie's conventional tie. Stan wore a flat-brimmed boy's Irish Derby hat (appropriate for his boyish character) and Ollie wore an English bowler. These became the key props in many of their gags. They both used a light pancake makeup to give them a more innocent look and Stan made his eyes look smaller by lining the inner lids.

It was not just in their own films that Stan and Ollie were portrayed in this way. They were usually drawn in similar garb in the Laurel and Hardy children's comic (which launched in 1955) and the related annual comic book which bore their name. They were also drawn that way in the British comic *Film Fun* (which ran for over 2000 issues) which carried a Laurel and Hardy strip. Similarly, almost all the many merchandising products as well as the toys, coloring books and the Laurel and Hardy cartoon series produced by Larry Harmon in conjunction with Hanna-Barbera in 1966 portrayed them in this way.

By the early 1930s, the Laurel and Hardy characters had developed into the form which made them internationally famous and successful. As McCabe puts it:

> They were, first of all, two supremely brainless men, totally innocent of heart and almost outrageously optimistic.... Certain gestures, movements, and spoken phrases became indelible trademarks: Stanley's armfold fall, his flatfooted walk ... his baby cry ... his elaborate head scratch which pulled up his hair to form a natural fright wig; Ollie's vast delicacy of gesture as seen in extended pinky and gracious hat tip, his embarrassed tie twiddle ... his look of exasperated frustration made directly to the camera following a Laurel misadventure, his imperious finger point to Stan either to remove his hat or his person elsewhere.... Ollie was "smarter" than Stanley yet he was infinitely dumber because ... he always thought he was smarter.... These two characters are the definition of friendship; living in a life framework of hopes perpetually deferred yet hourly renewed — the ultimate optimists. "Why don't you do something to help me?" Ollie asks Stan, who does — pushing them both therewith into a new catastrophe. The Hardy lament which most characteristically identified the team's essence is "Here's *another* nice mess you've gotten me into!" Those messes delighted millions, particularly during the Depression years when the troubles of the day were diminished by empathizing with the troubles of these two lovable dimwits... [McCabe, 2004, pp. 64–65].

Until the early 1930s, Laurel and Hardy made two-reelers. However, they were obliged to move into full-length feature films when fashion dictated that cinema audiences should no longer have one but two features films during an evening's entertainment. Other changes followed. The economics of making full-length films encouraged a less free and easy and more regimented regime at the Roach Studio and, as a result, Stan found it more difficult to control the way his films were made.

Laurel and Hardy's most creative period came to an end when they parted company with the Roach Studio and moved over to Twentieth Century–Fox in 1941. Relations between Stan and Hal Roach had been strained for some years. The rift seems to have developed particularly during the making of the feature film *Babes in Toyland* (1934). It was probably inevitable. Roach had bought the film rights to Victor Herbert and Glen

MacDonough's operetta of the same name, featuring a bizarre conflation of characters from children's stories in a production with more than a passing resemblance to a classic English pantomime. He is then said to have penned what he considered an improved story for the film and presented it to Stan. Inevitably influenced by his familiarity with the English pantomime tradition since his boyhood, and early theatrical experience with a juvenile pantomime company, Stan had other ideas on how to make the film. But even when Roach grudgingly yielded to Stan on the creative side of the production, the clash between them rumbled on. Henry Brandon, who played the classic pantomime villain in the film, recalled, "Roach and Laurel were arguing constantly while it was being made. Roach would tell Laurel his suggestions on the comedy scenes and they'd go into Roach's office and yell at each other. It was a real battle of egos. But Laurel got to do things his way" (quoted by Skretvedt, 1987, p. 290).

There would also almost certainly have been other clashes over the mounting costs of the production. *Babes in Toyland* was no cheap and cheerful short. It ran for 90 minutes and Roach's considerable facilities were inadequate to film such an extravaganza. Additional generators and hundreds of extra lamps were necessary to light the huge and complex 125,000 square feet of soundproofed set. The services of numerous independent companies were needed to provide the hundreds of elaborate costumes and 300 wigs which were looked after during production by a staff of 12 hairdressers. Even genuinely ferocious crocodiles six to nine feet long were employed, with armed guards standing by, as over 100 swimmers joined them in the water playing the role of "bogymen."[13]

Roach seems never to have forgiven Stan for the public injury to his pride, and the undermining of his authority in his own studio, during the filming of *Babes in Toyland*. The fact that Stan was so obviously vindicated, when the film was released and it earned Laurel and Hardy the best reviews of their careers, must have been the equivalent of rubbing salt into Roach's already smarting wounds. According to Skretvedt, the basic problem in the Roach-Laurel relationship was that:

> Stan Laurel was an artist and Hal Roach was a businessman, although one who had a great sense of what made a good comedy. The troubles arose when Stan, a salaried employee, tried to assume more control over films Roach was financing — and when Roach disagreed with Stan, who was

under contract as a writer as well as an actor, over what constituted a good story for Laurel and Hardy [Skretvedt, 1987, p. 333].

Another source of contention was that Roach insisted on Stan and Oliver having separate contracts. As he explained in 1981:

It was much better not having them under contract as a team — for Hal Roach. The advantage I had was that they could not leave me as a team. I always had one of them under contract. So, when I made a new contract with Stan, I was at an advantage because Babe was already under contract [quoted by Skretvedt, 1987, p. 313].

Stan and Oliver had reasonable reason for concern over their Roach contracts. There was a period in 1937 when Roach chose not to renew them and, although he subsequently rehired them as a partnership; his conduct could not have endeared him to his most successful employees. Moreover, despite their popularity and the box office success that was virtually guaranteed for any Laurel and Hardy film, they were not paid especially well by Hollywood standards. The fact that they were on salaries without any ownership rights in the films meant that they received no additional income when their films were shown on TV in later years: nor was any money paid to them or their estates when the films were released on standard and Super 8 film, VHS tape and DVD in the years that followed. In marked contrast, Charlie Chaplin secured a stake in his films from the outset and kept a tight rein on how they were re-released in later years. Whereas he retired to Switzerland with as many as 13 servants to care for him and his family, Stan spent his retirement alone with his wife in a comfortable but modest apartment. Although a mischievous newspaper article quite wrongly implied that he was hard up, it is true that Stan and Charlie were not in the same financial league. That was not due to differences in their drawing power at the cinema so much as to differences in the nature of Laurel and Hardy's contracts. As a result of Laurel and Hardy being well-off but not wealthy, when Oliver Hardy had a prolonged illness near the end of his life, it seems that his house was sold to help meet the huge medical bills that his continuing care entailed. In 1958, Stan wrote to a friend who had also been receiving regular medical attention:

I sincerely sympathize with you in regard to the financial situation — thats the tragic part of it all. This same thing happened to Mr. Hardy, his illness cost over thirty thousand Dollars in 11 months, even lost his home, it had to be sold to pay medical expenses — its shocking to end up like that after all the years of hard work.

Another factor in the deteriorating relationship at the Roach Studio is that Hal Roach, Jr., was put in charge of the production of Laurel and Hardy's 1940 film *Saps at Sea*. Stan did not enjoy working for someone who, though inexperienced, still adopted an authoritarian approach on the set. So Stan was ready to move on when the receipts for the film proved disappointing (compared to their previous film for which Roach Jr. had not been responsible), and Roach allowed Laurel and Hardy's contract to lapse.

The 1940s: An Unsettling Decade

Laurel and Hardy parted company with the Roach Studio on April 5, 1940. They were never to know a comparable settled period on any film lot again. They next performed before a live audience in a charity performance. Their sketch was so well received that it was incorporated into a Laurel and Hardy Revue that went on tour towards the end of 1940. Plans to take the Revue to England were cancelled at the last minute because of something beyond everyone's control: the developing horrors of the Second World War. It was not a sensible time for anyone to attempt to cross the Atlantic. German submarines were sinking ships at an alarming rate. Nor was Britain an ideal place to visit. The bombers of the Luftwaffe were targeting Britain's cities with an appalling loss of civilian life.

It was the runaway success of a military-based comedy film *Buck Privates*, starring Abbott and Costello, the new kids on the block, which helped to convince Twentieth Century–Fox that they needed to sign Laurel and Hardy (initially for just one picture) to compete with Universal's comedy duo. Ironically, Stan had helped to make *Buck Privates* a success by advising the then novice film actors on material which they went on to incorporate into their movie (MacGillivray, 2008, p. 20).

Before returning to Hollywood, Laurel and Hardy took part in a second all-star revue, this time for charity on a military base in California — and received an equally enthusiastic response. They could scarcely have had a more reassuring demonstration of their continuing popularity before returning to the business of making films.

Stan looked forward to having the opportunity to try out new ideas at Twentieth Century–Fox. It was a bigger studio and he anticipated that there would be no more of the battles over storylines, editing or contracts that had plagued his later years with Hal Roach. It was not to be. Stan found he had much less control over his films than had ever been the case at Roach.

He soon learned that big was not beautiful. In his readiness to accept an offer from a studio prepared to spend more money on productions, provide bigger supporting casts and stronger scripts, he seems to have overlooked the associated disadvantages. The most obvious was that Fox did not have an established track record making film comedy. Stan may have assumed that this would work to his advantage and give him more creative control. However, compared to Roach, Fox was a model of business efficiency. It operated with a rigid division of labor. Writers, directors, editors *and actors* did their job and nothing else. There was no room for a maverick, master of all trades, like Stan Laurel. Everyone involved in the production would be at the planning meetings — but not the starring actors Stan Laurel and Oliver Hardy. They would not even be invited to the studio until a full script had been prepared and the production team was ready to start shooting.

It has been argued that the results of this approach are apparent in the quality of the Fox Laurel and Hardy films. The directors at Fox, it is said, simply did not understand the relationship between the Laurel and Hardy characters that had made them so popular with cinema audiences. Nor did they realize how much Stan's contributions, coupled with the sequential filming and ad-libbing, had contributed to their success with Roach. The Fox writers ignored Stan's insistence on the need to improve on gags which had emerged originally as part of a coherent story. At Fox, similar gags were inserted more or less arbitrarily into the scripts. There was no genuine regard for comedy comparable to the collective pride that had been evident at the Roach Studio. Provided the films made money, they were judged to be successful.

While all these things may be true, thanks to Scott MacGillivray's research into the films made in the 1940s, we now know that this generally dismissive portrayal of the Fox years is over-simplified. Other factors played their part. The most obvious is that the studio was facing a manpower shortage. Over 800 Fox employees were serving in the armed forces at the time. However, much more significant is that Fox's Laurel and Hardy's films were produced under Fox's regime for B rather than A movies.

Laurel and Hardy's designated producer was Sol Wurtzel, the head of Fox's B films division. Given that double-feature performances are a thing of the past, younger readers may not be aware that for many years picture-goers enjoyed two films when they went to the cinema: an A main feature and a B supporting feature. The fact that Wurtzel was the head of the B division represented more than a blow to Stan and Oliver's pride. It meant that their producer had a specific business-based brief: to make profitable films efficiently. Wurtzel's personality was ideal for his situation. He was an unapproachable, no-nonsense taskmaster, not the kind of man Stan could charm or shout down. In the case of Laurel and Hardy films, his job was to make films to compete with those of Abbott and Costello at Universal.

Given that Abbott and Costello's first film was *Buck Privates*, it is not surprising that Laurel and Hardy's first film for Fox, *Great Guns*, was also a military comedy.[14] It proved to be a great commercial success and was so well received by audiences that Wurtzel took the unusual step of thanking Stan and Oliver in writing for their "sincerity and cooperation" and expressed the hope that they would make many more pictures together (MacGillivray, 2008, p. 23). But, while the film's success must have been gratifying to Laurel and Hardy, and they agreed to a renewal of their contract, they could not have been happy continuing without any creative control over their work.

Before returning to the studio, Laurel and Hardy went on tour again, this time to head up a variety cast on a tour of army camps in Florida, Puerto Rico, Antigua, Santa Lucia, Trinidad and British Guiana. They were amongst the first entertainers to volunteer their services for the war effort and went on to do over 500 such shows for service personnel during World War II.[15] They returned to Fox to do a short propaganda war film before a ten-week tour of midwestern states with another Laurel and Hardy revue in early 1941.[16] That was followed by a goodwill appearance in a star-studded *Hollywood Victory Caravan* performance in Mexico.

Immediately afterwards, they returned to the Fox Studio. There could now be no doubt that they were filming in the wake of Abbott and

Costello. Their next film *A-Haunting We Will Go*, followed closely on the heels of Abbott and Costello's *Hold That Ghost*. The film did not even make sensible use of the established Laurel and Hardy characters. Instead of building a film around the Laurel and Hardy characters, they were merely slotted into it. Stan became disenchanted and detached, and immediately after filming their final scene left the set. He and Oliver then went on to Washington to take part in another Hollywood Victory Caravan. After introductions to the First Lady, Eleanor Roosevelt, at the White House, the tour visited 11 more cities across the country. Although the Caravan included Bing Crosby, Bob Hope, James Cagney, Merle Oberon and Groucho Marx, it was reported that Laurel and Hardy's sketch was the hit of the show. So, especially as they had not enjoyed their recent spells on the film lot, they must have been gratified that they were still so popular with live audiences. Predictably, *A-Haunting We Will Go* received mainly negative reviews, yet the film still made a profit. The names Laurel and Hardy alone were obviously enough to guarantee its success.

Laurel and Hardy continued to be in demand in 1942. MGM invited them to star in *Air Raid Wardens* and Twentieth Century–Fox also announced that they would return to them to make *Jitterbugs*. But, before starting either film, Stan and Oliver went on another cross-country tour as part of *Stars Over America*. Filming at MGM eventually started at the end of 1942 under the watchful eye of a dour technical advisor and a representative of the federal government's Office of Civil Defense, who were determined that there would be no lampooning of what they saw as the vital role of air raid wardens. The compromise reached was that Stan and Oliver would try to do their job but fail and, for that reason, be relieved of their responsibilities. A number of old Roach employees were engaged and the atmosphere on the set was more relaxed than it had been at Fox. Stan was even allowed to make suggestions. The eventual release suffered from what film buffs call MGM's stately pacing and the absence of background music but it made a healthy profit for MGM and its exhibitors.

Mercifully, when Laurel and Hardy returned to Fox, the two copycat Abbott and Costello films that had been provisionally chosen for them were dropped in favor of *Jitterbugs*. Laurel and Hardy were directed by a comedy film enthusiast who gave them more freedom, and the set was comparatively happy. The writer and director actively sought Stan's opinions and both Stan and Oliver enjoyed making the film — to such an extent that Oliver later listed it as one of the top five films of his whole career (MacGillivray, 2008, p. 93). The reviews were markedly better and the profits again very healthy.

The fact that Laurel and Hardy's Fox films were made by the company's B unit did not necessarily mean that they were always shown as B features in cinemas. Typically, they would still be seen as the prime attraction, either alone or as the top half of a double bill. For example, when *Jitterbugs* was premiered on Broadway, it was as a single feature A film. Laurel and Hardy must have hoped that their future films would have a comparable standing when Fox announced in 1943 that they would now only make A films. However, instead, they found that their next film, *The Dancing Masters*, was conspicuous by its absence from the A list. In the event, the wholesale repetition of old sketches, coupled with lackluster editing, meant that, in MacGillivray's opinion, it really was a B movie. So it must be a further testament to Laurel and Hardy's popularity that it was still a major success at the box office and the third highest earner for Fox that year. But that was small consolation to Stan Laurel who was embarrassed by the film and privately considered it the nadir of his 1940s work. "We tried to tell them, if a bad film makes money, what would a good one do ... [but] the producers slap down a long list of figures that say we were smash hits at the box office ... so why do we want to be writing our own stuff?" (MacGillivray, 2008, pp. 125, 127).

Their next film, *The Big Noise*, about a devastating secret weapon, had the dubious distinction of anticipating the nuclear bomb that brought the war in the Pacific to an end. It was followed by a second film for MGM, *Nothing But Trouble*. Again, the box office receipts were excellent though the critical reviews were mixed. Their final film at Fox, *The Bullfighters*, was another mixed bag. Fox put fewer resources into it but at least the working conditions were somewhat laid-back. The tough Sol Wurtzel was not involved and Stan was able to exercise more influence on the set. It was probably the nearest thing to a genuine creative challenge that he had enjoyed since leaving Roach. Although the film was given little publicity by Fox, like its predecessors it went on to do well ticket-wise.

With hindsight, it may seem obvious that the move from Roach was a serious mistake for Laurel and Hardy. Hal Roach had at least shared

Stan's love of comedy and gave him the freedom to develop scripts. In contrast, the executives at Fox seemed only to be interested in stock film ideas that were cheap to produce. Critics and aficionados are not unanimous in their views on these later Laurel and Hardy films. While McCabe went so far as to describe most of them as "artistic disgraces," others have argued that they have been too readily dismissed and do have genuine merit.

Even if Laurel and Hardy had stayed at Roach, and become reconciled with their former boss, there would still have been two significant problems to overcome. The first was financial. Skretvedt suggests that the pattern of Laurel and Hardy's careers is an example of the way in which film industry economics served to undermine creativity. The freedom that made their short films so successful had to be curtailed as Roach was forced by market forces to make more expensive feature films. As a consequence, he was obliged to exercise more executive control over their production. That was one of the key factors which provoked the clashes between Stan and Roach and it was those clashes which, in turn, led to Laurel and Hardy's transfer to Fox. At Fox, there was virtually no scope for Stan's creative talents except as an actor.

The second problem was that Stan's screen persona of youthful innocence became increasingly difficult to sustain as he aged. But, had he remained at a sympathetic studio, Stan's creative inventiveness would no doubt have enabled him to evolve the Laurel and Hardy screen characters in a way that would have extended their film careers. But, in a studio like Fox, that was obviously not possible. Laurel and Hardy and Fox finally parted company in 1945 when Stan and Oliver declined an invitation to sign a contract for a further five years.

In assessing this period in the careers of Laurel and Hardy, it must not be forgotten that most of the other former silent comic actors who had once been successful, had long since fallen by the wayside. Even the great Charlie Chaplin had been struggling since his United Artists studio had been forced into bankruptcy in 1930, to a large extent because of the protectionist policies of MGM, Paramount and Universal who had used their control over their distribution networks to block United Artists' films being shown in cinemas. To continue making films, Chaplin had to throw himself on the mercy of the very studios that had contributed to the downfall of United Artists, and his subsequent film output in this period was far from memorable. He went into a personal decline, along with his creative reputation until, ironically, he portrayed himself as a washed-up clown in the 1952 comedy-drama *Limelight*. It was at about the same time that Laurel and Hardy were invited to Europe to make *Atoll K*, a project which could have revived their flagging careers too — but which was instead undermined by a wide range of factors, including Laurel and Hardy's deteriorating health.

Europe Calls

After their disappointing years at Twentieth Century–Fox and MGM, Stan and Oliver embarked on a tour of UK variety theaters in 1947. They received a rapturous reception. On their return to the U.S., they received an offer to make a film in France, which must have seemed like a wonderful opportunity for the two aging comic actors to resume their stalled film careers. Instead, they found themselves making another film over which they had very little creative control — one which they would not have wanted to mark the end of their careers. Instead of a reinvigorating return to the screen, it was a debilitating personal ordeal, and, instead of a creative international triumph for Laurel and Hardy, *Atoll K* turned out to be what some critics regard as their worst film.

The full story of this close to cinematic debacle is told in meticulous detail by Norbert Aping in his book *The Final Film of Laurel and Hardy — A Study of the Chaotic Making and Marketing of* Atoll K. The problems faced by Laurel and Hardy in making the movie (released as *Utopia* in the USA and *Robinson Crusoeland* in the UK) relate to the tortuous way the script was developed; the complexities created by a less than well-organized international production; Stan's health problems and, finally, the chaotic way the completed film was marketed. Aping's book may encourage readers to re-evaluate the film that McCabe dismissed as "execrable" but probably the best that can be said of it is that it had unrealized potential. The fact that the plot was similar to the theme of the successful British Ealing comedy *Passport to Pimlico* is indicative of what could have been achieved. In both films, pieces of land are freed from normal government control; such a situation could have added a new satirical dimension to Laurel and Hardy's legacy. Alas, it did not.[17]

But, whatever the merits or demerits of the film, there can be no doubt that the making of it was grueling and debilitating for Stan Laurel — and a complete contrast with the fun and laughter they had enjoyed in their halcyon days with Roach. During the many long delays in filming, Stan must have often regretted his decision to leave Roach in 1940. The fact that two people, who had made so many people laugh so much over so many years, should have had to endure such unhappy circumstances at the end their film careers is a terrible irony. It is often said that there is a very thin line between comedy and tragedy. That line was crossed, in real life, during the making of Laurel and Hardy's final film. Stan's wife Ida's subjective account of the experience is valuable. She recalls that the film took very much longer to produce than they had been told. When Stan arrived in Paris, the producer informed him that they did not even have a story, so they had to sit around to wait for one to emerge. Eventually, Stan tried to force the pace by bringing in his own writers but still had to contend with the French writers whom he judged lackadaisical by his own exacting standards. When shooting eventually began, the cast did not include the French comedian Fernandel and Italian clown Toto whom Laurel and Hardy had been led to believe would feature in the film. It seems that shooting occasionally produced some wry amusement but was ultimately frustratingly slow. According to Stan's wife, the director, Joannon, dressed himself up like Cecil B. DeMille and strode around the set carrying a megaphone. She recalls that Stan remarked, "Joannon is funnier than the picture — although *that's* not saying a hell of a lot." She also recalls that Joannon liked to shoot water and once spent three days shooting a lake because it was the most photogenic lake he'd ever seen. She added, and one hopes in doing so that she exaggerated just a little, that if Stan wanted even a little prop, such as a pencil sharpener, they had to send to Paris for it.[18]

The situation deteriorated rapidly when Stan became ill. He began to suffer excruciating pain, made worse by the fact that they were working at insufferably high temperatures. It took what seemed a long time to diagnose his problem but, because the necessary surgery was complicated by his underlying diabetes, an operation was put on hold until a specialist surgeon became available. Following surgery, Stan returned to the set before he was fully recovered and then developed dysentery. By this time his weight had fallen from 165 to 114 pounds. From then on, he was only able to work for very brief periods. His gaunt appearance is obvious and striking from the very outset of the film and it took him many months to recover his health after shooting was over and he returned to the United States (McCabe, 2004, pp. 80–83).

The film ends, with tragic irony, when Oliver turns to Stan and for the last time on film utters the words, "Well, here's another nice mess you've gotten me into!" Stan responds with his characteristic whimpered cry before an iris transition ends the scene to the accompaniment of their signature cuckoo theme. In different circumstances, this scene could have been a fitting end to their careers. In reality the film *was* a genuine mess and both men must have bitterly regretted that they had ever agreed to make it, especially as, in doing so, they had missed an opportunity to make another film in Hollywood.

During 1950 they were offered parts in the lavish RKO film *Two Tickets to Broadway* and ought to have been back in Hollywood in plenty of time to start shooting it. The brainchild of Howard Hughes, it was scheduled to be RKO's Christmas week attraction in 1951. It could have given Laurel and Hardy a new lease on life, especially as RKO had an altogether better comedy track record than Twentieth Century–Fox. But, because their return was delayed, they had to be replaced.

After a lengthy period of recovery, Laurel and Hardy reappeared on the UK variety circuit in 1952 and again in 1953. Upon returning to the United States after their third 1953 tour, they appeared on TV in 1954 in *This Is Your Life. Atoll K* was eventually released in the U.S. as *Utopia* in December that year.[19] At that time there were plans, at an advanced stage, for them to star in a series of films for television. Initially, Roach Jr. had suggested 39 half-hour episodes to be filmed over nine months. Stan dismissed such an arduous schedule but negotiated a deal to make four one-hour color spectaculars (at a time when color was reserved for genuine "spectaculars"). It seemed that he was at last going to enjoy complete creative freedom for a series to be called *Laurel and Hardy's Fabulous Fables*, which would be loosely based on the British pantomime format with which Stan had been familiar from his earliest years in show business.

Stan's Final Years

Early in 1955, Stan wrote in a letter to a friend:

We are negotiating with Hal Roach Jr to make four one-hour films for TV & with added footage to be released abroad in the theaters. We have a meeting tomorrow at the Studio & it looks like we may close the deal.

Several months later, he wrote to tell the same friend that he had been in hospital after a mild stroke which

has delayed the Roach deal, altho' they know nothing of my illness, I do'nt want to make any commitment until I am in condition to go ahead with it. I am feeling OK, but still very weak & have to get my strength back.

He sent a similar but more explicit letter to another friend:

I had a stroke, my left leg & left arm was paralyzed for quite a while. As soon as I am ready & able, I have four feature films to make with Hardy, we are going back to our old Studio (Hal Roach) needless to tell you how happy I am — never thought I would ever work again.

Although Stan did eventually make a good recovery, he never did work in television. Laurel and Hardy made their final public appearance together in 1955, in a filmed insert for a BBC television program about a British variety organization, the Grand Order of Water Rats, in which they reminisced about their friends on the British variety circuit.

At about this time, Oliver Hardy went on what appears to have been a fad beetroot-only diet and lost 100 pounds to try to ameliorate his heart condition. Perhaps because of the diet and rapid weight loss, he had a severe stroke on September 12, 1956, from which he never recovered. Stan vowed that without his friend and partner he would never work again (although it has been reported that he did write some gags and sketches for fellow comedians). Oliver died on August 7, 1957. Because of his own continuing ill health, Stan's doctors insisted that he must not attend the funeral.

Towards the end of his life, Stan received two awards which must have given him great satisfaction because they represented the verdict of his peers on his contribution to the cinema. In 1961 it was a Lifetime Achievement Award from the Academy of Motion Picture Arts and Sciences "for his creative pioneering in the field of cinema comedy." Unfortunately, he was too ill to attend in person and Danny Kaye accepted the award on his behalf.[20] Then, in 1963, he received the Screen Actors Guild Life Achievement Award. Again he was too ill to attend. "I was of course not able to attend the Annual Dinner at the Beverly Hilton, so again Danny Kaye accepted for me, looks like its getting to be a habit (he accepted my 'Oscar'!)" Subsequently, however, he was presented with the award at his home by Charlton Heston and the then President of the Screen Actors Guild, Dana Andrews.

In his later years, Stan Laurel was the most approachable of all movie stars. His phone number was publicly available and he welcomed all sorts of visitors — fans as well as friends and celebrities. He was also a great letter-writer. He wrote not only to close friends and relatives but also in reply to the thousands of fan letters he continued to receive. When the English musician Texas Pete Shovlin came across an archive of Stan's correspondence, he was so touched by it that he wrote the song *Letter from Stan* as a tribute. Particularly struck by Stan's familiarity with current events in the northeast of England, he wrote it as if from Stan to an imaginary Mary from that area. It relates to the period immediately before and after Oliver Hardy's death. All that can be provided here are Pete's touching lyrics but, if you would like to hear him sing the song, it is available on two websites (Shovlin).

> Dear Mary, many thanks for your letter
> How are you and how's the old town?
> Did you see the folks there, down at Old Dockwray Square?
> Don't tell me they're pulling it down
> And I know I wasn't born there
> But Shields is where I belong
> And the new Wooden Dolly is kidding herself
> She's got nothing on the old one
> Chorus:
> It's too bad about the shipyards
> Did they close the Empire too?
> Did the newspaper men pick their pens up again
> Hope the boys find work pretty soon
> Dear Mary, thank you for asking
> Mr. Hardy isn't doing too well
> I'd give him your best, but he's been told to rest
> And I guess only time will tell

And you say your husband looks like me
How lucky can any guy get?
Did I tell you the joke about the bow legged bloke?
Can you still buy those mint black bullets?

Chorus

Dear Mary, the letters get harder
I'm ok, but slow on my feet
I imagine you cried, when you heard that Babe died
But he's free from his pain now at least
And the skies get grey around me now
I've lost half of all that I am
And as I sit here tonight, I'm starting to type
Your very last letter from Stan

Chorus

Stan Laurel lived on to 1965. He died a few days after a heart attack on February 23, and was a gag man until the very end. Just minutes away from his death, he said to his nurse that he wouldn't mind going skiing at that very moment. The nurse replied that she wasn't aware that he was a skier. "I'm not," said Stan, "but I'd rather be doing that than have all these needles stuck into me!" A few minutes later, when the nurse looked in on him, he was gone. At his funeral, Buster Keaton said of him: "Chaplin wasn't the funniest; I wasn't the funniest: this man was the funniest." But Stan had already had the last word and it applied, most of all, to the "deadpan" Buster Keaton. He had once quipped: "If anyone at my funeral has a long face, I'll never speak to him again!"

An Enduring Legacy

Laurel and Hardy were not only popular with film audiences throughout the world, they remain universally admired by the comic actors who have followed them. Only a small selection of the huge number of tributes and acknowledgments paid to them can be listed here. In a 2005 *Comedian's Comedian* poll conducted amongst 300 comedians, comedy writers, directors and producers for the UK's TV Channel 4, Laurel and Hardy were ranked top amongst double acts, and seventh overall. Given the poll's origins, the results were inevitably skewed towards UK and more recent comedians. Despite that, Laurel and Hardy were placed far ahead of more recent figures such as Ricky Gervais and Robin Williams, and others closer to their generation such as Bob Hope and Phil Silvers. It is also notable that the only other former silent comic actor on the list was Charlie Chaplin — and that Laurel and Hardy ranked as many as 11 places ahead of him.

The UK's most celebrated comedy pair, Morecambe and Wise, noted in the foreword to McCabe's biography of Stan Laurel, "We have always been fervent admirers of that incomparable comedy duo, Stan Laurel and Oliver Hardy.... We must have seen every film that Laurel and Hardy ever made, and our early comedy routines were very definitely influenced by them" (quoted by McCabe, 2004, p. x). Among today's comedy actors, Ricky Gervais is hugely successful and has won numerous awards on both sides of the Atlantic, including two Emmys. While receiving the Sir Peter Ustinov Comedy Award at the Banff World Television Festival in 2010, he too emphasized that the inspiration for his comedy came from Laurel and Hardy.

> Everything began and ended with Laurel and Hardy. It hasn't really been improved upon because they nailed the most important thing in comedy, which was empathy. You can't laugh at someone you don't like. The funniest person you know is not a comedian: it's a friend that you like. Laurel and Hardy had that because they are precarious [vulnerable?]. I wanted to hug them. In everything I've done, I think I've stolen something from Laurel and Hardy [Calgary Herald 16 June 2010].

Dick Van Dyke went even further and singled Stan Laurel out for particular praise. Like Buster Keaton before him, he maintained that Stan was the greatest of all film comedians:

> I consider Stan the greatest of all film comedians. The reason is a very simple one. First of all because he got more laughs, both as a performer and creator of gags, than almost anyone else in film comedy. Not even Chaplin gets as much laughter, pure laughter, as Stan does. Chaplin is great — a genius — but with Chaplin I can always see the technique showing. Lord knows it's great technique, and I admire it very much — but with Stan the technique never shows. *Never*. And that to me is proof that he is a better craftsman than Chaplin — an infinitely better craftsman [quoted by Nollen, 1989, p. 5].

The late great Peter Sellers even took a poster-sized autographed photo of his hero Stan Laurel with him wherever he traveled. Both the character and voice of Chance, the gardener in *Being There* (Sellers' penultimate film), was modeled on Stan. Sellers was nominated for an Oscar for that performance.[21]

It is not just other comic actors and comedians and an adoring public who have valued Laurel and Hardy's contribution to popular culture. The celebrated science fiction writer Ray Bradbury, who loves Laurel and Hardy films and described watching his heroes live on stage in Dublin as one of the happiest days of his life, features them in three of his short stories (Bradbury, 1988, 1996 and 2002). In the most recent, *The Laurel and Hardy Alpha Centauri Farewell Tour* they are re-created by advanced biological techniques, two hundred years after their death, to provide a cure for *The Loneliness*, an overwhelming depression which afflicts those who spend long periods in outer space. Laurel and Hardy's universal and timeless humor cured *The Loneliness* by transforming sorrow into joy and tears into laughter and so allowed mankind to continue its outward journey to the stars! Others have been so aware of their enduring appeal that the unmistakable images of Laurel and Hardy have been featured in many unlikely situations such as a film by the Italian Federico Fellini; an episode of TV's *The Simpsons* and advertising campaigns for several products. Laurel and Hardy were even adopted as the code name for a key part of Britain's early warning system against nuclear attack in the 1960s. An obviously "tickled pink" Stan wrote to a friend in 1960 to tell him that a Minister of the Crown had announced in the House of Commons that the new radar system project in Fylingdales, Yorkshire, which would tell the difference between a Russian missile and a meteor, was nicknamed Laurel and Hardy. Stan considered it something of an honor but had one amusing reservation: "I think it was a mistake to name it this — just on account of it having two electronic brains. Actually we did'nt have ONE brain between us!"

Although Laurel and Hardy made their last film in 1952, their names still conjure up such an iconic comic image of an inadequate couple creating chaos that "Laurel and Hardy" is close to becoming an idiomatic expression. Many people now refer to a couple being like Laurel and Hardy or a situation being like a scene from a Laurel and Hardy film. The imagery is so strong that not even words are needed. The most striking recent example of that is the poster in which the faces of Tony Blair and George Bush have been superimposed on a photograph of Laurel and Hardy following the controversial invasion of Iraq.

What is equally remarkable is the enduring interest in their lives and work. Their films, in one form or another, have never disappeared from the scene. Noting the continuing financial success of the Fox and MGM films in the 1950s, Roach re-released their older films when it became obvious that they too could still make money. MacGillivray has done a magnificent job of describing the immense complexities of the subsequent trading in the rights to Laurel and Hardy's films, from the 1950s to the present. As a result, their films have continued to be shown in cinemas, televised and released on home video (MacGillivray, 2008, pp. 173–87 and pp. 257–315).

More than two million copies of their films were sold on VHS and in 2004 virtually all their work at the Hal Roach Studios was released on DVD. In 2003, Granada TV broadcast a Laurel and Hardy documentary on national UK TV, introduced by the famous jazz singer and literary critic George Melly. New jazz scores to accompany three of Laurel and Hardy's silent films were written by Steve Bernstein and performed by his Millennial Territory Jazz Orchestra in New York and at the Barbican in London in 2008 to critical acclaim.

Throughout the world there are Sons of the Desert Tents (fan clubs named after a famous Laurel and Hardy film) which hold periodic national and international conventions.[22] The 2009 UK event was held in Morecambe, England, just a short time after the unveiling of a bronze statue of Laurel and Hardy (paid for by the Sons of the Desert) outside the impressive Coronation Hall in Stan's birthplace, Ulverston. Even in Bishop Auckland, where Stan lived for only for a short time, the local authority contributed to the cost of a bronze statue of him, in a central location, which was unveiled in 2008. Many websites are devoted specifically to Stan Laurel and to the Laurel and Hardy partnership. Memorabilia related to them still sells for substantial sums. Perhaps even more remarkable is that despite the fact that there are so many Stan Laurel signatures available on photographs, letters, theater programs and numerous other bits of paper in circulation, his signature is still in such demand that forgeries are not uncommon.

In the UK, where Stan was born and brought up, his life and work are of continuing interest to today's playwrights. Tom McGrath's *Laurel and Hardy* premiered in the UK in 1976; revived in the West End of London in July 2009; and went on tour in the UK and in the USA in 2010.[23] Alex Norton's *Stan's First Night* (1987) was presented by Scottish TV and he now has plans to produce a film based on the play, which will be shot in the recently refurbished Panopticon Theatre, Britain's oldest surviving music hall, where Stan performed in front of his father in 1906. The prolific North Shields playwright Tom Hadaway from Stan's boyhood home had his *Actors and Orphans* premiered in 2004 at the Tyne Theatre in Newcastle upon Tyne, not only near to Stan's boyhood home but in the same theater in which Stan himself appeared in 1909. Neil Brand's *Stan* (2006), shown on BBC 4, featured Tom Courtenay as Stan, at the bedside of his close-to-death partner Oliver Hardy. Mike Gallant's *One Night: Stan* premiered in 2006 and Bob Kingdom's *Stan Laurel: Please Stand Up* premiered in 2008. News also emerged in late 2009 that the Scottish actor Robbie Coltraine, perhaps most famous for his role as Hagrid in the Harry Potter films, is hoping to make a film about Laurel and Hardy.

This book too, in its modest way, is a tribute to Stan Laurel, who together with his partner Oliver Hardy brought laughter to millions in a period when, even in the developed world, there was widespread hardship and suffering. With one exception, his films were made in the United States. But his passion to make people laugh, and the initial development of his comic talent, developed many years earlier, over 5,000 miles away, in North Shields, a small riverside town in the northeast of England.

6

Echoes of a
North Shields Boyhood

In his poem "The Rainbow," William Wordsworth introduced the phrase, "The Child is Father of the Man." Whatever specific meaning he may have intended, the phrase is now used as an acknowledgment that what we experience when we are young has a lasting influence on what we value and appreciate for the rest of our lives. Applied in the specific case of Stan Laurel, it means not only that the nature of his boyhood would, inevitably, have influenced what he valued as a man; it also means that it would have influenced his approach to comedy. What this chapter sets out to demonstrate, in the *Stan's Approach to Comedy* section below, is that Stan's position at the Roach Studio allowed him a remarkable degree of freedom to impose his ideas both on the way in which the Laurel and Hardy films were made and on their specific content. Then, in the subsequent six sections, it sets out to illustrate ways in which his boyhood experiences, particularly those in North Shields, are manifest in the films which he had such a pivotal role in creating.

Stan's Approach to Comedy

Stan Laurel was not just a supreme comic actor. Indeed, as was noted in Chapter 5, his first sustained period of employment with the Hal Roach Studio was as a writer and director. He was still contractually tied as an actor to another film producer; it was on the strength of his growing reputation as a creator of comic situations and gags that he was signed by Hal Roach. So when he began to work at the studio in 1925, shortly before his 35th birthday, it was behind rather than in front of the cameras. Amongst other films, he directed several featuring Oliver "Babe" Hardy before their careers began to coalesce on screen. However, even when he returned to his original role as a comic actor, he continued in his role as director and writer and was the key, creative figure behind the Laurel and Hardy films.

When Stan joined the Roach Studio it already enjoyed an unparalleled reputation for comedy, based on two-reelers (films 20 to 25 minutes long) which it churned out at an astonishing speed.[1] Yet, despite this exhausting schedule, Stan relished the opportunity he was given by Roach. He explained to his biographer John McCabe that at the Roach Studio he had joined a group of men who rejoiced in the creation of comedy and that, despite all the hard work, "It was like a perpetual party." He added: "I can't think of a better life than just making comedy, or when we weren't doing that, just sitting around and thinking and planning comedy" (McCabe, 2004, p. 56). Even while making a film, they would still take advantage of breaks in the shooting to relax together. Roy Seawright, the optical effects man at the studio recalled that when things were quiet, they would roll a piano onto the set and Leo McCarey would play while Stan, Oliver, Charley Chase and Leo would sing. He expressed regret that no recordings were made of these impromptu musical events:

> You'd walk in and listen to them, and you'd be entranced. The whole studio would come to a complete stop, the minute word got round that they were singing. People would just flock around that stage. Stan and Babe and the others would have a whole group watching them and they'd be completely oblivious to it. My God, how they harmonized; they all recognized each other's talent, and they loved it [quoted by Skretvedt 1987, p. 59].

In conventional film studios such as MGM, Universal or Twentieth Century–Fox, describing someone as a director would provide a good indication of their actual role in the making of a film. Although film directors varied in their preferred approach and how much latitude they were allowed by the film's producer, they were the key creative force behind the films they made. Sometimes, the director was free to select both actors and key crew members, such as those behind the camera. In other instances, the director had to work with those they were given. Nevertheless, in the typical studio it was the director who was ultimately responsible for the storyline, the set design, the choice of lighting and the camera angles. After shooting, it was the director who was ultimately responsible for the editing of the raw footage and post-production effects, such as music. In short, it was the director's role to determine how a film should look and feel.

Roach, however, was not a conventional studio. The actors did not stick to the credited writer's script and the credited director did not provide firm guidelines for the actors and technicians. In fact, very often the credited writers and directors did not play a particularly active role in the production of a film. In the case of the Laurel and Hardy's films, the key creative figure was always Stan Laurel. This important conclusion was reached by Randy Skretvedt after a large number of interviews with those involved in making their films. In addition, he emphasized that the whole pattern of making Laurel and Hardy films deviated from the established pattern because Stan's way of making film comedy was based on his own theatrical experience. Ordinarily, actors would stick to the script that had been written for them and the director would expect both the actors and the technicians working on the film to follow the guidelines determined for each sequence. That often meant that many takes were made of each scene until the director was satisfied with the result. Since this was a time-consuming process, and most of the film shot ended up on the cutting room floor, compensating economies were achieved by shooting the film out of sequence, with all the scenes at a given location shot at the same time.

Almost the opposite guidelines were followed when Laurel and Hardy films were produced at the Roach Studio. Stan and Oliver routinely deviated from the script even though Stan had already been involved in writing it. Instead of the director being in charge, it was Stan who directed the actors and technicians — and even the credited director. Crucially, in order to try to achieve spontaneity, there was usually only one take of each scene. Whenever possible, they also filmed the sequences in the order in which they would appear in the final film, not least because no one could know in advance how much Laurel and Hardy's ad-libbing would change the scripted story (Skretvedt 1987, p. 49).

Stan explained something of this in a 1960 interview with Larry Goldstein. The credited director, Stan explained, was merely an overseer who kept the production under a modicum of control:

> We just shot the film with a mere outline of the story and gags. As the film progressed, the director would suggest a new line which we might try out and then either keep or reject. There was a constant emphasis upon spon-

taneity in the filming — the director or stars would ask each other, "Is this funny?" or "How would this look?" and propose a stunt they thought could be incorporated into the action [Stan Laurel Correspondence Archive Project].

Anita Garvin, who appeared in 11 Laurel and Hardy films, suggests that Stan's relationship with the credited director on the film was sometimes a subtle one, which almost invariably resulted in things being done his way.

A lot of directors thought that they were directing Stan but believe me, Stan was the one who was directing. And the director was never cognizant of the fact. Stan was clever; he had a brain, in spite of that look. He would make suggestions in such a clever way. He'd say, "You started to say ..." and the director thought it was his own idea. He'd suggest different things to actors too. He'd say, "How do you think this would work?" He wouldn't tell you what to do but he'd ask your opinion. And 99 percent of the time you'd say "Great!" because he had a comedy mind like no one I have ever known before or since [Skretvedt, 1987, p. 61].

The inevitable conclusion that Stan was the *de facto* director of the Roach Laurel and Hardy films is also supported by the fact that though they had two dozen credited directors over the period, "the films have no discernible stylistic differences" (Skretvedt, 1987, p. 65). The same cannot be said of the films made later at Twentieth Century–Fox and MGM when Stan lost creative control.

At Roach, Stan set out to approximate the experience of a live theatrical performance and knew just how he wanted the films to look on screen. He demanded bright, even lighting in each shot so that if he and Oliver began improvising and moved to another part of the set while the cameras were running, they would still be consistently lit. He also allowed for the time a large cinema audience would laugh at a gag by introducing pauses in the action — just as a music hall or vaudeville artist would wait for the laughter to subside before continuing. If, during a preview of a film, they found that they had judged the pauses incorrectly, "Stan would decide what to cut. Nobody interfered with what he wanted" (Bert Jordan, long-time Roach editor, quoted by Skretvedt, 1987, pp. 69–70). It was because of those carefully constructed pauses that Stan considered the films unsuitable for television without further editing. The contagion of laughter in a large cinema audience was not replicated in a small family living room.

Stan's role as a writer continued after he returned to acting. As

Skretvedt explains: by 1929 Stan was "basically the head writer; he took the gag men's ideas, added his own, and distilled them into the final script." Leo McCarey, who more than anyone else was responsible for bringing Stan back in front of the camera in tandem with Oliver Hardy, was fulsome in his praise for Stan's talents as a comedy ideas man and insisted that "Stan had one of the best and most inventive comedy minds in history" (McCabe, 2004, p. 62). The extent of Stan's creative contribution to the Laurel and Hardy films was summed up by Hal Roach when discussing the credits that appeared on the screen. "If you had everything on the screen that Laurel does, his name would be on there about ten times" (Skretvedt, 1987, p. 346).

Emphasizing the key role played by Stan in creating both the Laurel and Hardy characters and their comic situations is not in any way to belittle the contribution of Hardy to the success of the partnership. He was a superb comic actor in his own right. Hardy was not a straight man to Laurel. His contributions on screen matched those of Laurel. They were a genuine team: each needing the other and each contributing to the laughter. Both could ad-lib and had an unerring knack of knowing just how to play a scene to bring the best out of one another. Off-screen, however, it was a different story. When the day's shooting was over, Oliver went off to relax. At that point, Stan's key additional behind-the-scenes roles began all over again. And on the set the next day, it was Stan who was ultimately responsible for directing operations whoever happened to be sitting in the director's chair. Stan was a man with a vocation. He was dedicated to creating situations which would make people laugh.

This difference between the way in which Stan and Oliver approached the making of films at Roach does not mean that Oliver lacked the experience or ability to play a more creative role in the process. Earlier in his career, before he teamed up with Stan, he had also played a multiplicity of roles. As his wife Lucille explained to John McCabe:

> Everybody helped everybody in those days. The cast helped the crew when making set-ups and the crew helped the cast — many times acting as background extras when needed. Babe, for instance, many times during filming worked in turn as script clerk, assistant cameraman, assistant director, and once in a while during emergencies even became the director. So, he learned the motion picture business from the ground up, although he always preferred to be in front of the camera [McCabe, 1976, p. 71].

It was not because Oliver lacked creative ability that he left things to Stan. It was rather because he recognized Stan's unique talents and was happy to defer to him. According to Lucille:

> He had a great admiration for and complete confidence in Stan's ability for "feeling" comedy situations and constructing them.... Even when he felt inside himself that something wasn't just right ... he felt that if the thing was wrong, Stan would see it eventually and put it right.... And, true to Babe's predictions, Stan would suddenly see on his own the faults Babe had talked about and then he'd work out a solution to the problem [McCabe, 1976, pp. 88 and 89].

Considerable academic analysis has been devoted to the kind of talent with which Stan was so richly endowed, i.e., the ability to create situations which make people laugh. In his important book *The Act of Creation*, the philosopher Arthur Koestler argues that, amongst all the creative acts, laughter is particularly amenable to such systematic analysis precisely because "humour is the only domain of creative activity where a complex pattern of intellectual stimulation elicits a sharply defined response in the nature of a physiological reflex" (Koestler, 1964, p. 96). However, such deep analytical exercises with respect to comedy would not have been appreciated by either the screen persona Stan Laurel or the real life, off-the-screen Stan Laurel. Try to imagine a situation in which Stan and Ollie are on screen in conversation with Arthur Koestler. The smart intellectual Koestler is trying to explain to the dumb comic actors Stan and Ollie, how it is they have succeeded in making so many people laugh for so long. Without uttering a single word, Laurel and Hardy would have been able to turn such a situation into a wonderfully funny screen moment. As Koestler offers them the substance of his profound intellectual analysis, anyone at all familiar with Stan and Ollie on screen will be able to visualize how, by the use of just a few familiar facial expressions, exchanged glances and embarrassed body language, they would have had audiences howling with laughter as the needlessly wordy Koestler used hi-falutin' language to try to explain what makes people laugh.

> The pattern underlying all varieties of humour is "bisociative" — perceiving a situation or event in two habitually incompatible associative contexts. This causes an abrupt transfer of the train of thought from one matrix to another governed by a different logic or "rule of the game." But certain emotions, owing to their greater inertia and persistence, cannot follow such

nimble jumps of thought: discarded by reason, they are worked off along channels of least resistance in laughter [Koestler, 1964, pp. 96–97].

The real-life Stan would have been no more appreciative of Koestler's attempt to understand his art. It seems likely that he would have dismissed it with a brief and less than polite expletive. All he and the others at the Roach Studios did, he would protest, was do their best to make people laugh. As McCabe (who came to know Stan so well) explains, "Stan had no philosophy of comedy, and he regarded any attempt to define one on anyone's part as a pretty amusing joke in itself." What Stan did emphasize, however, was that Laurel and Hardy comedy contained an element of sympathy that was absent from the "common slapstick" of the Keystone Cops or the Three Stooges. He also suggested that experience with live audiences was a key element in the development of successful screen comedy. He once said to McCabe:

> Never, for God's sake, ask me what makes people laugh, I just don't know. To get laughs you simply have to work hard all the time and learn how to do it in your bones. You can't do that until you get a lot of experience before live audiences. Audiences are strange things. I love them but sometimes they are hard to figure out [McCabe, 2004, p. 172].

Stan was undoubtedly right. Audiences are hard to figure out. But so too are the comic geniuses who find ways to make audiences laugh. And, whatever gives them that ability, the fact remains that Stan and his co-writers and directors off screen, and Stan and his partner Ollie on screen, found ways to make millions of people forget their troubles and laugh at the situations they created on film. Given the frenetic pace and the team approach which characterized the making of films at the Roach Studio, there is little point in trying to identify which individual was responsible for any particular idea. That said, and with Stan such an influential and inventive member of the team, it would be surprising if his boyhood in North Shields did not in some way impact on the comedy situations he had such a key role in developing. Indeed, in a letter to a correspondent which has already been quoted above, Stan listed some of his boyhood escapades, then quipped that they were the foundation of his film character. He also mentioned in his 1957 interview with Arthur Friedman that he sometimes consciously slipped in pieces of dialog which he knew would be particularly appreciated by English audiences. So, while it may not be possible to demonstrate with absolute certainty that his life in North Shields provided the direct and conscious inspiration for any of the films he helped to create, it is certainly probable that the memories of his boyhood years did contribute to the films he made during his career in Hollywood.

By the time that the Laurel and Hardy characters had become established on screen, they had become known as "the Boys." Nollen insists that this is not a coincidence. He argues that it is a perfect way to describe the characters of Stan and Ollie who are physiologically men but psychologically children. He adds that in several films Stan struggles to read, write or even tell the time (Nollen, 1989, p. 40). Hardy made a similar remark when he suggested that "one of the reasons people like us ... is because they feel so superior to us. Even an eight-year-old kid can feel superior to us (quoted by Nollen, 1989, p. 35). Nollen went on to argue:

> The Boys literally are just boys, children who attempt to act like mature human beings.... Like the behavior of young children who try to emulate grown-ups, each instance in which either of them attempts to perform as a mature person is quickly transformed into a total disaster. At times, they begin to participate in mature activities ... but do not possess sufficient development and experience to bring them to a successful conclusion.... Stan is like a child who is still learning by imitation and cannot grasp abstractions or make any jump in reasoning [Nollen, 1989, pp. 35–36].

Many similar instances can be cited of the way in which Stan's screen persona, in particular, resembles that of a boy. In *Brats* (1930), in which Stan and Oliver each play the role of both father and son; they are afforded a unique opportunity to act the parts of boys as well as boy-like men. In the film, the resemblance between Stan the boy and Stan the man goes beyond that of them looking alike. For example, his lack of guile in the way in which he plays checkers (draughts) is evidence that he has yet to develop the poker face for games which comes with maturity. The film also contains examples of Stan's frequently used device of rendering common adult expressions incorrectly. After Oliver shouts at the children, Stan rebukes him, "Don't talk to them like that. Treat them with kindness. ... Remember the old adage, 'You can lead a horse to water but a pencil must be lead.'" Despite Stan's garbled rendition of the adage, Oliver nods his assent and says, "I guess you're right." What is noteworthy is that Oliver always seems to understand Stan's confused utterances, in much the same way that older brothers and sisters can often understand their younger siblings when grown-ups cannot.

Numerous other instances could be cited of Stan's boy-like difficulties with common adult expressions: his request for a room with a southern *explosion*; his remark that he has heard that "the ocean is *infatuated* with sharks"; his telling a distressed Oliver that it is "no good crying over *split* milk" and that, when Oliver seems to need spectacles, he should go to see an *optimist*. In other instances, Stan uses a variant on the device. He renders an expression more or less correctly the first time but then mangles it hopelessly when asked to repeat it. Perhaps the best known example is in the opening sequence of *Towed in a Hole* (1932): "You know, Ollie, I've been thinking. I know how we could make a lot more money." "How?" "Well, if we caught our own fish, we wouldn't have to pay for it, then, whoever you sold it to, it would be clear profit." "Tell me that again," says Ollie. This time, much more hesitantly, Stan explains: "Well, if you caught a fish, and whoever you sold it to wouldn't have to pay for it, then the profits would go to the fish...." At this point, conscious that he is confused, Stan stops. But Ollie sums it up succinctly: "I know exactly what you mean. Your idea is to eliminate the middle man."

Stan's whimper when things go wrong is comparable to the response of a small boy who has yet to develop an adult response to a situation that he has found overwhelming. His problems with physical coordination and even his surreal white magic (such as being able to ignite his thumb as if it were a lighter) can also be construed as further examples of the boy in Stan the man. In the former, they are examples of what he is not yet man enough to accomplish. In the latter, they are examples of what his boyish imagination still allows him to believe may be possible.

Stan's boyish screen persona surfaced long before the advent of the Laurel and Hardy partnership. For example, in *Dr. Pyckle and Mr. Pride* (1925), the parody of *Dr. Jekyll and Mr. Hyde* made for Joe Rock, the most heinous things that Stan gets up as the fiendish Dr Pyckle are boyhood pranks: stealing a small boy's ice cream; firing his pea-shooter at several people, and blowing up and bursting a paper bag behind an unsuspecting lady.

Nollen suggests that Stan's psychological screen persona is comparable to that of a six-year-old boy (Nollen, 1989, p. 36). I do not think it is possible to be so precise. All I would suggest is that Stan's boyish screen persona approximates to the boyhood years he spent in North Shields. They were certainly eventful years, with the potential to provide memories to last a lifetime. In 1897, shortly after he arrived in the town, a mighty storm destroyed a 300-yard length of the just completed pier at the entrance to the River Tyne, leaving the lighthouse marooned. In 1900, torrential October rains produced such widespread flooding on Tyneside that even the steep roads close to his Dockwray Square home were underwater. The year 1901 saw the death of Queen Victoria, who had been on the throne since 1837, the longest reign of any British monarch. But it was probably in terms of technological change that the period was most memorable. The start of the twentieth century ushered in the age of electricity and Stan was a boy in North Shields at the very time that electricity ceased to be a novelty and began to dramatically transform the lives of ordinary people. The town's first electrical works opened not far from his Dockwray Square home in 1901 and the first electric tram ran past his father's Theatre Royal later in the same year. In 1902, the stage at his father's Theatre Royal, like that of the Boro' Theater, was lit by electricity for the first time. Two years later, North Shields became part of the first electrified railway line in the whole of the UK. Interestingly, an electrical store was the focal point for the film *Tit for Tat* (1935); it sold not only easily broken light bulbs but also a range of the electrical household gadgets that had become available since his boyhood. The piece of white magic employed by Stan in *Great Guns* (1941) also had an electrical dimension. It involved him unscrewing a light bulb which then remained lit as he held it in his hand.

Stan's boyhood years were heroic in many other respects. In 1901, Marconi transmitted his first wireless message and in 1903 Orville Wright made the first successful controlled flight in a powered aircraft. Cars, though still a novelty, began appearing on the streets. Olds set up the first production line to manufacture cars in the U.S. in 1902 and motor taxis were introduced to the streets of London in 1903.

However, it is not just major events which loom large in our memories of our childhoods. So too do the sights, sounds, smells and personal events which (though seemingly trivial to adults) can stay with us for the rest of our lives. We know from Stan's letters, interviews and public statements that he remembered a great deal about his boyhood. Given that Stan played a pivotal role in the creation of the Laurel and Hardy films, it would be surprising if those boyhood experiences in North Shields did not resonate in many different ways in the films he went on to make in faraway Hollywood. There are at least eight such possible echoes of North Shields which demand consideration: steep flights of stairs, fish, ports, ships, sailors, collars and ties, soot and alcoholic water.

Steep Flights of Stairs

Originally, as was noted in Chapter 2, North Shields consisted of no more than a narrow strip of land that ran alongside the river. For obvious reasons it became known as the Low Street. It was there that North Shields Fish Quay, as it is known today, was constructed in the 1870s, not many years before Stan came to live in the town. On a steep cliff above the riverside is the Bank Top where Stan's home in Dockwray Square was located. So although Stan lived just a stone's throw from the riverside, his house was about 70 feet above it. To get from one to the other, the most direct route was to use one of the many sets of steep stairs that had been cut into the bankside. The climbs up these stairs were memorably arduous. Steep roads did exist at either end of the long Low Street up to the Bank Top above. However, if one wanted to deliver something to the houses that were built on the bankside itself, there was no alternative but to use the stairs. In other words, what one had in North Shields, and virtually on Stan's boyhood doorstep, was an almost identical location to that used by Laurel and Hardy in their Oscar-winning film *The Music Box*.

Anyone familiar with North Shields Fish Quay will have seen those flights of stairs running from the riverside to the Bank Top — though far fewer will have actually climbed them. As someone who, like Stan, has climbed them on many occasions, I can assure readers that the experience is not easily forgotten. In Stan's day, there were even more such stairs than there are in the same area today. In an as yet unpublished book on the stairs, Jack Shotton lists as many as 29 sets of stairs and banks. Quoting from a 1941 document, he notes that the very long Low Street had only four "outlets for vehicular traffic" but that there were many other means of entering and leaving the Low Street:

These were the stairways which ran amongst the picturesque red-tiled or thatched buildings on the steep bankside. Some of them made a bee-line, as though to reach the top as quickly as possible, some wound from side to side in a leisurely walk, while others seemed to lose breath half-way and, becoming discouraged, vanished in the wilderness of bricks and mortar and never emerged from the depths; and most of them sent off little branch stairways and lanes and left and right at every conceivable angle [Shotton, 2006].

Over the years since Stan left North Shields, many of these stairs have disappeared. Several were lost when the bankside was cleared of housing in the 1930s and others were demolished or covered when it was decided that the bankside should be further tidied up in the 1960s. However, it is readily obvious from the several stairs that do remain that they are all capable of conjuring up the kind of images portrayed in *The Music Box*, one of the greatest comedy films in cinema history. The fact that the stairs led to and through the overcrowded bankside dwellings in Stan's day means that he would have actually seen furniture being carried up and down the stairs. There may well have been alternative ways to deliver to his home in Dockwray Square but the stairs represented the only route for any deliveries that had to be made to the dwellings built on the bankside.

It is highly likely that, in one way or another, Stan's experience of these flights of stairs played a part in the evolution of the plot for *The Music Box*. The idea of delivering something awkward and heavy up such a long flight of steps was used in two Laurel and Hardy films, the silent *Hats Off* (1927) and *The Music Box* (1932). Both films were shot on a flight of steps running off Vendome Street in the Silver Lake area of Los Angeles — a longer but similar set of stairs to the several which Stan would have climbed as a boy in North Shields. In 1927, Laurel and Hardy delivered a washing machine up the steps: in 1932 it was a piano.

While visiting North Shields during the preparation of his book *Laurel and Hardy. The British Tours*, A.J. Marriot was struck by the remarkable similarity between the Ropery Stairs and *The Music Box*'s Silver Lake Stairs. Aware that this may have provided the inspiration for the film, he has subsequently provided a Dockwray Square–based speculative account of how the idea for the film might have emerged. Marriot, himself a comedian, invites us to imagine that:

Once upon a time, a removal man was making a delivery to Dockwray Square. He couldn't find his way in so asked some local kids. "It's up the top of them steps" they told him. Seeing no roadway he staggered up the steps with his wares. When he got to the top the kids met him and said, "Mister, why didn't you drive your horse and cart around, and come along this road here?" Stan may or may not have been one of the boys, but he knew of the story. It would have been a source of local humour for years after. Fast-forward twenty-seven years. Stan tells the story around a table full of gag-writers, after which all would agree it would make a good short.

Marriot readily concedes that his is a speculative exercise but maintains that, even if someone else from the Roach Studio initially conceived the idea for the film, the first thing that would have struck Stan is how much they resembled the North Shields stairway and that his mind "would not have had to go into overdrive trying to think how he could make a funny situation out of them" (Marriot, *Step by Step*).

I am not persuaded that any particular flight of stairs provided the likely direct or indirect inspiration for Laurel and Hardy's antics on the Los Angeles *Music Box* stairs. As the images below illustrate, even today there are several flights of steep stairs in North Shields which closely resemble those used in that film. However, what I do share is Marriot's conviction that there is in *The Music*

North Shields High Beacon stairs.

Box a very strong echo of an area of North Shields very close to Stan's boyhood home. What I would also suggest is that steep flights of stairs are just one of many echoes of North Shields in the films of Laurel and Hardy.

Fish

Stan lived his early life in Dockwray Square, immediately above the Fish Quay at a time when the fishing industry was at its peak. In 1876, landings of fish at North Shields were in the region of 370 tons. The advent of steam trawlers and other innovations in the industry sent the catch soaring to around 13,000 tons when Stan lived in the town.

In 1904, just before Stan left for Glasgow, there were 143 first-class fishing vessels registered in North Shields, in addition to many other second- and third-class vessels. Countless other fishing boats landed their catches at North Shields, although registered at other ports (Craster 1907, p. 304, and Wright, 2002, pp. 14–18).[2]

The most successful of the fishing entrepreneurs was Richard Irvin, who had occupied 8 Dockwray Square before the Jeffersons moved in. He was born in North Shields in 1858 and steadily built up a huge international business empire. By the closing decades of the 19th

North Shields Nater's Bank stairs.

century, fish were being landed at North Shields in quantities far in excess of local requirements. To preserve them for use elsewhere, herrings were smoked and sold as kippers — along with smoked haddocks and bloaters. Gutted and cured herrings were packed into barrels. In 1901 the Shields Ice and Cold Storage Company was built to enable fish to be kept fresh for sale in more distant markets. However, even with ice readily available, the supply still exceeded demand and large quantities of fish were sold to a local factory to make fertilizer. Irvin then decided to add a cannery (known locally as the tin factory) to his variety of methods for preserving fish for sale in towns and cities far beyond North Shields.

Los Angeles *Music Box* stairs. (Courtesy of *Downtowngal,* who has generously made the photograph freely available to all via Wikipedia under the Creative Commons Attribution–Share Alike license.)

To look down on all this frenetic activity related to fishing, the young Stan Jefferson had to do no more than walk a few yards from his home. If he chose to climb down one of the flights of stairs to the quay-side, he would have found himself in the midst of all that activity. So, as Stan grew up, unlike the vast majority of other English children of his age, he was familiar with the sights and sounds of fishing boats being built and repaired; with hundreds of fishing boats going to sea and returning with their abundant catches. He would have watched the fish being landed; packed for delivery to other parts of the country; gutted, cut into suitable sizes for sale, smoked to make kippers, a then favorite breakfast food, or canned in Richard Irvin's "tin factory." While Stan lived in Dockwray Square, he was never far from fish markets, fish shops and fish sellers, who walked around local streets selling the day's catch, attracting the attention of customers with their characteristic musical cries. He would also have been familiar with the tempting smell of deep fried fish and chips; the unpleasant smell which clung tenaciously to those who had been handling "fresh" fish and the awful smell which emanated from the guano works where unwanted scraps of fish

North Shields Library stairs.

were transformed into fertilizer — an issue his father vowed to try to alleviate when he was first elected as a councilor in 1901.[3] Stan even fell into a barrel of fish guts as a boy, a memorable event which he told many people about in later life. He must also have spent time in the nearby fishing village of Cullercoats (an area of the Borough of Tynemouth for which his father was an elected councilor). At the time it was famed for its crabs which were sold directly from the fishermen's cottages or from the creels (large wicker baskets) of the Cullercoats fish lasses who had been made internationally famous through the paintings of the celebrated American artist Winslow Homer, who lived in Cullercoats in 1881 and 1882.

In short, fish figured prominently in Stan's life in North Shields. Fish also featured to an unusual extent in the films Laurel and Hardy made as compared to the films made by their contemporaries (e.g., Charlie

Chaplin) and successors (e.g., Abbott and Costello). That is obvious from the section *Fish* in Glenn Mitchell's *The Laurel and Hardy Encyclopaedia*.

> Stan and Ollie sell [fish] in *Towed in a Hole* and catch them in both *The Laurel-Hardy Murder Case* and *The Live Ghost*. The latter instance is all the more pointed for their supposed profession of gutting them [for a living: "We clean fish over at the fish market"], as they do also in *The Flying Deuces*. Caveman Stan clubs fish into submission in *Flying Elephants* but in the solo film *Bears and Bad Men* his best catch is a pair of corsets. Stan and Ollie attempt to grill a fish over bedsprings in *Bonnie Scotland*, a film where snuff induces a Hardy sneeze sufficient to drain a river, leaving its finned inhabitants in dry dock. Another unfortunate specimen is confined to a small tank in the laboratory of Professor Noodle in *Dirty Work*. Bigger fish stand more of a chance, notably the shark in *The Flying Deuces*. Another resilient breed, shellfish, are represented by the runaway crab from *Liberty* and Stan's pet lobster in *Atoll K.* One of the early Warner Brothers cartoons caricatures Laurel and Hardy as fish, something that clearly failed to diminish Laurel's off-screen fondness for deep-sea angling. On a post-war visit, one journalist noticed Stan's lapel badge,[4] earned in 1935 after landing a 256-pound tunny [actually, a marlin] [Mitchell, 2008, p. 107].

North Shields Ropery stairs.

Some of these examples warrant elaboration. Stan is found fishing for something much less ambitious than a 256-pound marlin in the opening scene of the 1930 *Laurel-Hardy Murder Case* (an incidental scene not directly relevant to the plot of the film). He and Oliver are sitting on the edge of a wooden quayside. Oliver is asleep but Stan is fishing with just a weighted and baited line (as did countless children in North Shields — myself included). After Stan catches a fish and frees it from the hook, he puts it down under Oliver's bottom. It wriggles and wakes him up. Subsequently, Oliver persuades Stan to wind up his line (in the self-same way I was taught to do as a boy) and move on. Laurel and Hardy also start the 1934 film *The Live Ghost* fishing on a quayside. This time Stan is fishing with his line attached to the slim branch of a tree, again in the same way that children do.

It is a crab which prompts most of the gags in the silent film *Liberty* (1929). Laurel and Hardy play escaped convicts but, in the confusion to change from their prison garb into their civilian clothes, they put on each other's trousers. Most of the rest of the film revolves around them trying to find a sufficiently private place to correct the situation. The key trigger for most of the comedy action comes after they attempt to change behind some wooden crates of fish lying in ice outside a fishmonger's side entrance. Before proceeding, Stan pauses to pick up a fish and returns it to the crate. He then smells his now "fishy" fingers and grimaces. As he drops his trousers, a live crab from the crate behind him falls into "his" (but in reality Oliver's trousers). Startled by the fishmonger, they then hurry off, still in the wrong trousers. The subsequent sequences, including the mass breakage of '78 records, are all precipitated by Stan's erratic movements as the crab keeps nipping him from behind. Eventually, they manage to change trousers on the top of the steel structure of a multi-story building site. However, the crab moves along with the trousers so it is now time for Oliver to start jumping erratically, in an altogether more dangerous situation. Even after Oliver discovers the crab and removes it, it still takes center stage again as it scuttles along a girder and nips his now bare toes.

A quite different passing reference to fish comes in the closing sequence of *Way Out West* (1937). On leaving Brushwood Gulch with Laurel and Hardy, the heroine declares that she would like to go home to the south. Oliver responds in his best Southern accent, "Well, honey, we'll all go down to Dixie. Oh for a slice of possum and yam" [a traditional Southern dish]. Not to be outdone, Stan adds: "Yes sir, and some good old-fashioned fish and chips. I can smell them from here"—only to be interrupted by Oliver with a dismissive "Fish and chips!"

In fact, Hardy, like Laurel, very much enjoyed English fish and chips which were then usually bought from shops which served nothing *but* fish and chips. Unlike the dish of the same name served in restaurants in the United States, the English version involves one large (rather than several small pieces of) fish, deep fried in batter and served with English chips — which are bigger than French fries and not remotely like American chips, which the English call crisps. After being seasoned with salt and malt vinegar they were and still are wrapped in paper (newspaper in Stan's day) and often eaten outside with the fingers. Stan's wife told John McCabe about one particular incident when he fancied some fish and chips while playing one of the less salubrious theaters into which they had been booked when their 1947 UK tour had been extended by popular demand.

> It was a really dirty, draughty old theater [in Bolton]. Stan wanted to send out for some fish and chips. Stan adored fish and chips. But the stage door-keeper protested — he said indignantly that fish and chips would smell up the place. Stan just looked at the man, and took a deep breath, getting that backstage air in his lungs. "Bring the fish and chips please," he told the man politely. "They'll be like perfume to the air floating round in here"[5] [Marriot, 1993, p. 20].

Among the surviving Laurel and Hardy scripts is a fragmentary outline written by Stan. It is undated. Skretvedt believes that it is an embryonic version of the plot of 1932's *Towed in a Hole* (Skretvedt, 1987, p. 249). George Marshall, one of Stan's co-writers, claimed the credit for the opening scene of the film, in which Laurel and Hardy are driving around the streets trying to attract the attention of potential customers for the fresh fish they have on sale. I have no reason to doubt that claim but Stan's boyhood memories of all things related to fishing would have undoubtedly influenced the way in which he subsequently developed the idea and devised the film's gags. It is also worth emphasizing that the film was made in 1932, just months after Stan and Oliver's return from a visit to North Shields.

The film begins with Hardy singing "F-r-e-s-h f-i-s-h! Caught in the ocean, this m-o-r-n-i-n-i-n-g" while Stan is tooting casually on a short brass fish horn. Hardy would no doubt have relished the opportunity to use his fine singing voice in this still early sound film and Stan, as a boy, would have been familiar with just such street traders' cries — of which fish traders' cries were by far the most numerous. Those common in and around North Shields had been collected in 1924 by Robert King (in *Old Tyneside Street Cries*).

"If we caught our own fish," Stan suggests to Oliver, "we wouldn't have to pay for it." Hardy responds favorably to the suggestion and they buy a dilapidated old boat and start to repair it. Predictably, they are conspicuously unsuccessful. Whether or not Stan had seen similar mishaps in real life to those he helped create on screen we will never know but what he *had* seen could certainly have provided some of the inspiration for the comedy setting and gags. Although North Shields was never as important a shipbuilding town as its close neighbors Howdon and Wallsend, it did enjoy a modest share of the shipbuilding activity on the river, which was given an impetus by the boom in the fishing industry which developed in the second half of the 19th century. Stan would certainly have seen similar small boats being built and refurbished in his boyhood. The type of boat built most often by smaller shipbuilders was the Northumbrian Coble, a 20–25 feet long ft fishing vessel. According to Wright, "The shipyards on the River Tyne turned them out at an amazing rate" (Wright, 2002, p. 18).

Ports, Ships and Sailors

North Shields may have been best known as a fishing port but it was also the scene of much more extensive maritime activity. Moreover, given its position at the entrance to the Tyne, it was an ideal viewing point for the boats and ships entering and leaving the river. Stan would have been able to see them all from the Bank Top by Dockwray Square. Today, when it is possible to stand there and see no more than an occasional ship entering or leaving the river, it is difficult to appreciate the sheer scale of activity that existed in Stan's day. As well as coastal shipping in British waters, trade was carried out from the Tyne with many international ports. In addition to the coal-carrying colliers, merchant ships carried other cargoes into and out of the river. Other ships left the Tyne after having been built at yards on the river, including the *Carpathia* (1902) which picked up survivors from the *Titanic*, and the *Mauretania* (1906) which was close to completion when Stan left for Glasgow; it went on to hold the Blue Riband for the fastest crossing of the Atlantic for many years. The fishing boats, the local river traffic of tugs, ferries and dredgers, the ships coming into the river for repair and those leaving it after having being built or repaired as well as the vessels of the Royal Navy, must also have left a lasting impression on the young Stan Jefferson. So too must the sights and sounds of the quayside below Stan's home where we know from his own accounts that he spent a lot of time as a boy.

It is certainly the case that ports, ships and sailors appear in many Laurel and Hardy films. The whole of the 1936 *Our Relations* takes place on the quayside of a port not unlike North Shields. The married, landlubber brothers Stan and Oliver have lost contact with their single, twin brothers, Alf and Bert, who ran away from home and went to sea. When Alf and Bert come ashore (from the *Periwinkle*), in the very port where the married Stan and Oliver live, there is ample scope for a plot based on mistaken identity. The bars and lodging rooms are reminiscent of the riverside of a town like North Shields, and even the expensive night club and restaurant in the film is designed like a sailing ship, down to the rigging (which they climb), which we know Stan was familiar with from the *Wellesley* Training Ship which was anchored in the river just below his home.

The opening sequences of *The Live Ghost* (1934) are shot in quayside bars and on the quay of a port. To make some easy money Laurel and Hardy agree to help shanghai a crew for a ship with such a bad reputation that it is known to local seamen as a "ghost ship." After knocking out the sailors as they leave the bar and handing them over, Laurel and Hardy then find themselves in literally the same boat with a resentful crew waiting for an opportunity to take revenge on the pair responsible for their fate. The closing sequences are shot in another port, "ten ports later."

Why Girls Love Sailors (1927) begins with shots of cargo being loaded onto the *Merry Maiden* and the whole of the rest of the film takes place in a quayside town. Stan, a periwinkle fisherman, saves his girl from a proverbial fate worse than death at the hands of the *Merry Maiden*'s wicked captain, after a chase in which he becomes entangled in fishing nets.

As I have already noted, the opening scene of *The Laurel-Hardy Murder Case* takes place in a port. Stan is fishing from the edge of a wooden quayside against a background of cut timber comparable to that which was landed in North Shields from the Baltic ports. Behind the timber are

View east from the Bank Top by Stan's Dockwray Square home, showing the Wellesley Training Ship and river beyond, as well as the crowded bankside and riverside houses immediately below Stan's own elegant and comfortable home. The Low Street is so narrow that it is obscured by the buildings. (North Tyneside Local Studies Library.)

the masts of ships accompanied by the occasional sound of a ship's horn. The same scene was used at the start of the Spanish film *Noche de Duendes* (which is actually a composite of two of their films, *Berth Marks* [1929] and *The Laurel-Hardy Murder Case*).

Two Tars (1928) begins with actual footage of the U.S. Navy fleet at sea and shots of sailors disembarking. Our heroes are described as "two dreadnoughts from the battleship *Oregon*." Their escapades lead to a long line of cars being damaged in their efforts to impress the two young ladies they have picked up. The talkie equivalent *Men o' War* (1929) is confined to a public park and its boating lake, much like the Tynemouth boating lake with which Stan was familiar as a boy. The theme is once again two sailors on shore leave, trying to impress the two young ladies they have picked up.

The Making of Stan Laurel

Mitchell's *Laurel and Hardy Encyclopaedia* provides us with yet more examples of boats and ships in the films of Laurel and Hardy:

> The sea-faring twins of *Our Relations* arrive on board the *Periwinkle*, a craft only slightly more reputable than the reputed ghost ship in *The Live Ghost*. Even more decrepit is the tiny *Prickly-Heat*, aboard which Stan and Ollie become *Saps at Sea*. It does at least prove seaworthy, which cannot be said of the *Momus*, which founders in a storm early in *Atoll K*. When attending a convention in *Sons of the Desert*, the boys are unaware that the ship on which they are supposed to be has foundered. *Why Girls Love Sailors* survives in a French version titled *There Was Once a Little Boat*; another smaller craft is filled with water to detect leaks in *Towed in a Hole....* In *Nothing But Trouble* they return by sea to a wartime America, having been released by the Japanese (who prefer ritual suicide to Ollie's cooking!). Another 1940s exploit, *Jitterbugs*, concludes with a river-boat chase. *Sailors Beware* is a tale of intrigue set aboard the cruise liner *Mirimar*, the same ship that brings Stan to America in *Putting Pants on Philip*. Other trans–Atlantic trips are implied in *A Chump at Oxford* and *The Flying Deuces*.

Just as boats and ships must have loomed large in the experiences of the young Stan Laurel, so too must the sight of sailors in uniform. In addition to the sailors who docked at North Shields, Stan was also familiar with the sight of boys of his own age in naval uniforms. The huge *Wellesley* Training Ship anchored in the River Tyne, like other such ships elsewhere in the UK, catered for boys from workhouses, waifs and strays and others judged to be delinquent in some way. It provided them with training so that they would make ready recruits for the Royal and Merchant Navies. The T.S. *Wellesley*, which was originally the wooden battleship *HMS Boscawen*, had accommodation for 300 boys, admitted between the ages of 11 and 14 years, and was a certified Industrial School. The trainees featured prominently in events in the town, for example, in the Relief of Mafeking celebrations in which Stan also played a significant role.

Given Stan's familiarity with ships, sailors and sailors' haunts (of which a great many existed on the Low Street in North Shield), it comes as no surprise that they too are featured prominently in Laurel and Hardy films. As Mitchell notes:

> *Sailors Beware* takes place aboard a cruise liner, with Ollie as Purser and Stan as a shanghaied steward. Both he and Ollie are shanghaied in *The Live Ghost*. *Any Old Port* chronicles their adventures ashore after a whaling voyage, while *Our Relations* presents the boys' seafaring twins, Alf and Bert.

122

Stan and Ollie take to the high seas accidentally in what is supposed to be a moored boat in *Saps at Sea*. They join the U.S. Navy in *Two Tars* and *Men o' War* (Stan had also worn naval uniform in his 1925 solo film *Navy Blues Days*). Another representative of that service crops up in *Angora Love*. The systematic destruction of Ollie's suits in *Helpmates* obliges Ollie to meet his wife in an Admiral's costume. This is the most prestigious moment in the team's nautical career, unless one counts the time in 1947 when Stan joined the crew of HMS *Dolphin* in queuing up for the rum ration.

As I have argued with respect to the striking similarity between the steep flights of stairs Stan knew as a boy in North Shields and the stairs used for *The Music Box*, my suggestion is not that any particular boat, ship or sailor provided the direct inspiration for any of the boats, ships or sailors portrayed in Laurel and Hardy's films. What I do suggest is that the sights and sounds of boats, ships and sailors which were so familiar to him as a boy would almost certainly have fed at least indirectly into the creative processes that generated the situations and gags for many of Laurel and Hardy's films.

Collars and Ties

On screen, Laurel and Hardy usually wore wing collars. In Stan's case, his wing collar was accompanied by a bow tie. The extant photos of Stan's father show him also wearing a wing collar and bow tie. The similarity is unlikely to be a coincidence. However, whereas in the case of his father the wing collar and bow tie were an indication that he was an elegant, well-dressed man, in the case of Stan they were a comic item: an incongruous accompaniment for a man who, far from being elegant, was wearing an ill-fitting suit and literally down-at-heel shoes.[6]

As a boy, Stan obviously did not wear the wing collar, which was usually a fashion accessory for a man wearing a tailcoat, dinner jacket or morning suit. What he did wear as a young boy was the large soft collar and elaborate tie which was popular in the late Victorian period and became known as the Buster Brown collar. Worn often in conjunction with an elaborate coat and hat, it was an outfit that would make any self-respecting boy cringe if photos of him in the garb were to be shown to his friends in later life. Subsequently, Stan graduated to a hard starched Eton collar and suit. The Eton suit is a curious example of a school uniform which became a fashion item for boys who did not attend the school. Adapted from the uniform of the famous public (i.e., private) school Eton College, the outfit had by the Edwardian era been adopted by many aspiring middle-class families as Sunday best wear for their sons. The Eton collar was particularly popular with parents (but not their sons) even when the rest of the outfit was not adopted.[7]

Irrespective of their age, until they reached a height of 5 feet 4 inches, Eton pupils were obliged to wear a short jacket known as a bum-freezer and the broad, starched Eton collar. Winston Churchill's grandson (also called Winston), who attended Eton in the mid–1950s, recalled in his autobiography that, because he was amongst the smallest boys in the school, he was required to wear a short Eton jacket together with a broad and most uncomfortable starched collar for much longer than his taller friends. Anthony Armstrong-Jones (now Lord Snowdon and the former husband of Princess Margaret) never did graduate to the Eton tailcoat because he was still too small for it when he left the school. The discomfort of wearing the Eton collar has also been recalled by the Duke of Beaufort who remembers having to wear "an abominable Eton suit with a big, stiff and desperately uncomfortable collar."[8]

The starched Eton collar was no more popular with the young Stan Jefferson. Horace Lee, who was managing director of the North Shields Theatre Royal, recalled Stan as a little boy, visiting the theater with his mother and sister Beatrice. "In those days he was dressed in the orthodox Eton collar, black coat and grey trousers. He particularly hated the collar" (*Shields Daily News*, October 12, 1933). Lee had made a similar observation to another journalist in 1931. He noted how Stan used to stand in the wings fingering his collar and complain: "My mother will have me dress like this!" (*Shields Daily News*, June 12, 1931). When, according to Stan (in a letter written later in his life), he fell into a barrel of fish guts on the fish quay, he was wearing his best Sunday, i.e., Eton suit. On another occasion, while again dressed in his Sunday-best Eton suit, he was hit with a soot bomb thrown by (to use his words) "a street urchin."

Given my argument so far, it would be surprising if Stan's large soft and hard starched collars and Eton suit did not figure in some way in one or more of his films and there are two instances in which they do — quite apart from all the others in which Stan's neck gear is the same as that worn by his father.

In *Brats* (1930), in which Laurel and Hardy play the roles of both adults and their lookalike sons, it is poor young Oliver Hardy who has to wear something comparable to the embarrassing large soft collar and elaborate neck tie worn by Stan when a very young boy. Stan, however, is dressed more agreeably in a sailor suit of the kind worn by the boys on the Wellesley Training ship. Such suits had become particularly popular after they had been adopted for Queen Victoria's own boys by her husband Prince Albert, as part of their rigidly controlled childhoods which were intended to instill in them the importance of discipline and duty. It is noteworthy that, although *Brats* was made in 1930, and Laurel and Hardy as adults were dressed appropriately for that period, the outfits worn by Laurel and Hardy as boys had long since gone out of fashion. What they wore is reminiscent of the Victorian period when Stan was growing up in North Shields.

The Eton suits and collars had to wait until *A Chump at Oxford* (1940). Laurel and Hardy are cast as a pair of street-sweepers who inadvertently stop a bank robber from escaping. Asked to name their own reward, they request an opportunity to have a

Photograph of Stan Jefferson as a young boy, wearing a large soft collar and elaborate necktie remarkably similar to that which Oliver wore in *Brats* (1930). The collar and tie have been outlined because this photograph (more than 100 years old) is now faded and worn. (With the kind permission of Nancy Wardell [Stan Laurel's cousin].)

proper education and are sent, all expenses paid, to Oxford University in England. For a reason not immediately explained in the screenplay, they arrive at the University dressed not like the other undergraduates but in Eton suits with bum-freezer jackets. In short, they are incorrectly dressed for Oxford and for Eton (because they are both well over 5'4"). "So this is Oxford" comments Oliver. "Yes, I think we're going to like it here," responds Stan. They are then approached by an undergraduate who asks, "Pardon me, but haven't you come to the wrong college." "But this is Oxford, isn't it?" Oliver asks in response. "Yes, but you're dressed for Eton" replies the student. Oliver then provides the audience with the reason why they are inappropriately dressed by pointing the accusing finger clearly at Stan: "It's your idea us being dressed like this. No wonder everyone's staring at us."

It seems very likely that it really was Stan's idea for Laurel and Hardy to dress in something akin to the outfit he so disliked as a boy. He knew it would make them stand out from the crowd and, from his own personal experience, help represent them on screen as potential victims—not in this instance for a well-aimed soot bomb from a boy on the Fish Quay at North Shields, but the practical jokes of the students of Oxford University.

Soot

The experience of being hit by a soot bomb obviously stayed with Stan for the rest of his life. He remembered exactly where he was when the incident occurred, and that he was dressed for a birthday party in his best Eton suit. He not only referred to it in letters to correspondents but also recalled it to an audience of 1,400 in the Gaumont Theatre in North Shields in 1952, when he took to the stage during a charity concert. For the benefit of readers brought up with central heating systems who have never seen soot, I should explain that it is the plentiful, intensely black, soft powdery carbon residue left behind in chimneys when coal fires are burned. In the days when almost all homes were kept warm by coal fires, it was necessary to occasionally remove it not only to help fires burn and allow the smoke to escape easily up the chimney but also to ensure that

An artistic impression of an advertisement for *A Chump at Oxford* (1940) in which Laurel and Hardy are wearing conspicuous and out-of-place stiff Eton collars and short "bum-freezer" jackets at Oxford University. Stan detested having to wear an Eton suit and collar when young, not only because of the discomfort but because it made him a target for pranks by other boys.

the chimney did not catch fire and that there were no falls of soot from the chimney into the room below. When that happened, as it did from time to time if the chimney was not swept regularly, the intense black soot would billow from the fireplace and cling tenaciously to all of the furniture, carpets and rugs that it touched.

Chimneys were cleaned with a series of special, inter-connected, long-handled brushes. Stan would have seen chimney sweeps around the streets

This is the narrow street in North Shields, as it looked in Stan's day, where he was hit by a soot bomb while wearing his "Sunday-best" Eton suit. It is obviously not an easy place from which to make an escape. The Wooden Dolly appears as it did during most of the time Stan lived in North Shields. (Courtesy of North Tyneside Local Studies Library.)

of North Shields (who, no matter how careful they were, always bore the sooty tell-tale signs of their trade). He would also have experienced periodic visits from a sweep to clean the chimneys in his own home. At the time Stan arrived in North Shields we know from Ward's Trade Directory that at least five firms of chimney sweeps were active in the town. The work of the chimney sweep was always fascinating for children, not least the sight of the brush finally appearing from the chimney, an image which was used to such good effect in the film *Dirty Work*. Just as *Towed in a Hole* followed shortly after Stan's visit to North Shields in 1932, so too did *Dirty Work* (1933), in which Laurel and Hardy play chimney sweeps, with predictably disastrous results.

Soot also features in *Me and My Pal* (1933) when Stan suggests to Oliver (playing the part of a groom late for his wedding because everyone around him is preoccupied with a jigsaw) that he should hide up the chimney when a fight breaks out. Predictably, when he emerges his face is covered in soot. Soot also features in *Laughing Gravy* and the similar but not identical sequences in the French film *Les Carottiers* and the Spanish film *Los Calaveras*. In all three, Stan and Oliver hide their dog from their landlord on the roof via their chimney. In due course, Stan follows the dog up the chimney and emerges onto a snow-covered roof covered in soot. Oliver in turn climbs up on the roof from their upstairs window and then all three of them return to their room via the chimney. For the remainder of the subsequent lengthy sequence they remain covered in soot while the process of washing it off provides the source of a further series of gags.

Oliver also finishes up covered in soot in *Hog Wild* (1930), when he falls down the chimney during an unsuccessful attempt to fit a radio aerial to his roof. It may be two other characters who finish up covered up in the comparable coal dust in *Sailor Beware* (1927) but it is Stan, the acting steward, who is given the job of bathing the dirty child (who is actually a dwarf, adult thief). Scenes involving soot were also scripted for other films, e.g. *Brats* (1930) and *Helpmates* (1931), but not included (Skretvedt, 1987, pp. 191, 225).

Alcoholic Water

In a letter to a correspondent in 1955 (quoted in the next chapter), Stan explained that his father decided to send him, as a boarder, to Tynemouth College because of his "always being in mischief and trouble at home." At the end of a list of escapades he added: "Think this was the forerunner of my film character!" The final example which he quoted was "drinking gin (thought it was water)" which made him "cockeyed," i.e., drunk.

That was precisely the pivotal gag of *Scram* (1930). After Laurel and Hardy are ordered to leave town because they are vagrants, they are befriended by a drunk who takes them "home." The drunk leaves alone when he discovers he is in the wrong house — but not before he has poured a large jar of bootleg gin into a water jug. When the lady of the house faints on seeing the strangers Laurel and Hardy in her home, they pour her a glass of water from the jug. Predictably, she becomes drunk and decidedly giggly. The film ends when her husband (the judge who earlier had ordered them to leave town) returns home to discover the three of them in an innocent but apparently compromising position. Two years earlier, in *Blotto*, the same gag had been given a reverse twist when Stan and Oliver behaved as if they were drinking illegal alcohol when, in reality, they were drinking a vile non-alcoholic concoction which Stan's wife had substituted for the real thing.

The pivotal theme of Laurel and Hardy's 1934 short *Them Thar Hills* is an elaboration of the drinking scene in *Scram*. Oliver is recommended by his doctor to take a trip into the mountains and advised to drink plenty of fresh water. He and Stan rent a trailer and arrive in an isolated area just after a group of locals have been discovered by the police and obliged to dump their barrels of moonshine (illegally brewed strong liquor) into the well. When Stan draws water from the well, he notices its distinctive color and "tickly" taste but Oliver attributes this to the iron in the water. "That's why the doctor told us to drink plenty of it. Try some; it's good for your nerves." Stan takes a liberal ladle-full and remarks, "I feel better already." They follow the doctor's advice to drink plenty of it and are soon relaxed and happy. By the time a husband and wife stop by, hoping to borrow fuel for their car, Stan and Ollie's speech is slurred and it is obvious that they are drunk. When the wife takes a drink of water, she remarks that it is delicious. When her husband declines to follow her example, she tells him: "Okay, baby — you don't know what you're missing!"

While the husband takes fuel to the car, Stan, Oliver and their visitor continue to follow the doctor's advice — with increasing enthusiasm. By the time the cold sober husband returns, his wife is also gloriously drunk and carousing happily with Stan and Ollie. He is not amused and, in the inevitable row that follows, there is a wonderful tit for tat exchange which finishes up with Oliver having the seat of his trousers set on fire. At Stan's suggestion, Oliver jumps into the well to quell the flames only to find that the alcoholic well water explodes and he is sent flying into the air.

Stan becoming "cockeyed" features in other Laurel and Hardy films. In 1933's *The Devil's Brother* (also known as *Fra Diavalo*) (1933) and 1936's *The Bohemian Girl* he gets drunk by imbibing the remaining "surplus" alcohol when the containers he has been given to fill can hold no more. In *Swiss Miss* (1938), he becomes drunk by fooling a St. Bernard dog into letting him drink the contents of his barrel of brandy.

I do not claim that this chapter contains a definitive list of the echoes of Stan's North Shields boyhood which can be discerned in the gags and situations that he helped to create on film. It seems likely, for example, that the way in which Stan rushes around telling people "There's going to be a fight" in *Block-Heads* (1938) is based on one or more actual boyhood incidents since that was exactly the way in which news of an impending fight in a schoolyard was broadcast to the rest of the boys. Other clues may exist in letters I have not seen or in the recorded remarks he made to others that I have not encountered. However, there are enough examples here to convince me that Stan was making more than a flippant quip when he suggested to a correspondent that his boyhood escapades may have been the forerunner of his screen character. His remark also implies that he was conscious of a connection between them. That is not to suggest that he deliberately sought to recreate on film events which he had witnessed or participated in during his youth. But it is to argue that echoes of his boyhood are there to be seen on screen and that Stan's boy-like screen persona was no mere coincidence. When we are young and inexperienced, our best endeavors can turn out very differently from the way we expect. When we are also naïve and innocent, those unanticipated mishaps can produce reactions in others that seem utterly disproportionate and bewildering. Imagine an image of Stan, scratching his head in disbelief at the mayhem that has followed his best-intentioned endeavors and it is not difficult to also visualize a young boy wondering why on earth he is in such trouble when he cannot even begin to understand what he did that caused events to go so awry. It is perhaps because so many film-goers worldwide could remember their own childhood escapades that they were able to empathize with the antics of Stan and Oliver on screen. Laurel and Hardy may have looked like two grown men but it was in large part because they behaved so much like naïve young boys that their films proved to be so compelling and funny.

We must be grateful that the young Stan Jefferson could not have been paying attention in church when the text of the sermon was: "When I was a child, I spoke as a child, I understood as a child, I thought as a child: but when I became a man, I put away childish things" (St. Paul's Letters to the Corinthians, 13:11).

7

Lifetime Links with North Shields

Stan lived in California for very much longer than he lived in North Shields. Had he distanced himself from his roots, as so many successful people have done, his memories of his boyhood home might have faded completely. Yet it is obvious from his many letters that the memories of those formative ten years stayed with him all his life and that North Shields always occupied a warm spot in his heart. As an old North Shields pal, Sylvester Blackett, recalled in 1990, "Stan was a lifelong friend from teenage days up to the time he died in LA ... Stan often used to mention some of our old friends in his letters to me — like Horace Lee, Roland Park, the photographer, a nutcase we had in Shields we used to call 'Happy Ralph' and 'Dance for a penny Bob' as well as some of the grand comedians the Tyne produced."[1]

Stan described his time in North Shields as the happiest days of his life and used to refer to it affectionately as "the old town" and said that he felt that he *belonged* to it even though he had been born in Ulverston and lived for so long in California. He visited it three times during his trips from the U.S. to the UK and stayed in touch with residents until his death in 1965. Psychologists tell us that reinforcement is the key to memory. Stan's prodigious appetite for letter-writing meant that he received continual reinforcement of his boyhood memories. His inventive mind and innate comic wit continually conjured up images of how new developments were changing the town when he learned of them from friends and fans. One obvious example is to be found in a letter, quoted below, in which he conjured up the preposterous image of the sex-symbol Marilyn Monroe as the model for the new North Shields "Wooden Dolly," with a tank on her back containing live herrings. At the time he left the town, the Wooden

The replacement Wooden Dolly at the time Stan left North Shields. The unidentified boy in the Eton collar is *not* Stanley Jefferson. (North Tyneside Local Studies
Library.)

Stan during his retirement years in the 1960s, at his desk by his typewriter. (Courtesy of Bernie Hogya and the Stan Laurel Correspondence Archive website.)

Dolly was a carving of an elderly North Shields fish hawker with a large wicker basket on her back containing dead fish. Another example is his observation that the then-new pedestrian tunnel under the River Tyne sounded so posh that you would have to wear your Sunday best to walk through it.

Many of Stan's letters were handwritten; still more were bashed out on his faithful long-serving typewriter. Those letters currently available through the Stan Laurel Correspondence Archive website and others already published elsewhere make fascinating and revealing reading. They include many references to North Shields and further evidence of the extent to which there were echoes of the "old town" in his thoughts, even half a century later, when he was living 5,000 miles away in the sunny southwest of the United States.

Some of his references to Shields are poignant. In 1932, after his planned quiet visit to the town had turned into a flight from the media and an adoring public (see the next chapter), he wrote to one correspondent:

> Thanks for mentioning my little Brother's grave — I thought of it while I was there, but was unable to go where I wanted to go, my whole time was taken up with Public — Press — & Photographers. I went over for a rest — but came back a nervous wreck.

Stan's five-month-old brother Sydney Everitt had died in 1899 when Stan was nine years old. However, the reference to Sydney's death and grave at this particular time would have had an even more emotional significance for Stan than is evident from this extract alone. On May 7, 1930, just two years before his return visit to North Shields, Stan's only son Stanley Robert Jefferson had been born two months prematurely and had died after just nine days. His body was cremated because, it has been suggested, Stan found burials particularly distressing. One inevitably wonders if his feelings towards burials may have been influenced by the early experiences of his brother's burial at the age of 9, and his mother's, when he was 17.

Other letters show a mixture of poignancy and happy nostalgia. By the time Stan returned to North Shields in 1947, the town had been pounded by the bombs of the Luftwaffe during the Second World War and still bore the scars. He mentions this in the following handwritten letter from the Savoy Hotel in London:

> Dear ...
>
> Please pardon delay in reply to your very sweet letter — greatly appreciated & certainly brought back many memories to me.
>
> Yes, my Dad is still living — saw him a month ago — 85 now.
>
> When I played Newcastle — I took a ride around No. Shields — it was sad to see the old Town in such a State — but I got a thrill just the same to see once again Dockwray Square — Saville St etc. I didn't see the wooden Dolly — But asked after her & understand the old Gal is still there! Will close now — Many thanks for writing — it was a great pleasure indeed to hear from you among my many friends in the North — with kind regards to self & family — Trust alls well & happy with you —
>
> Bye now & God Bless —
>
> Sincerely —
>
> *Stan Laurel.*

Stan's many affectionate references to the Wooden Dolly in his letters requires some explanation. It stood at the entrance to the Custom House Quay, on the riverside Low Road, not far from his Dockwray Square home. The original Wooden Dolly was the figurehead from a collier brig. When the owner's son, David Bartleman, was killed in 1791 while trying to fight off a privateer, the figurehead of the ship was removed and positioned in the front garden of his parents' home as a memorial. In 1814 it was moved to the Custom House Quay, close to the river's edge, and became the first Wooden Dolly. For some reason, given the fate of Bartleman, a tradition developed in which many seamen (who are notoriously superstitious) cut off a sliver in the belief (or vain hope) that it would keep them safe at sea. The first Wooden Dolly was replaced by a comparable figurehead in 1850. That was replaced by the third Dolly, another ship's figurehead, in 1864. By the time Stan arrived in the town circa 1895, it had been so disfigured that a stream of letters to the local newspapers demanded a replacement. When Stan was 12, and probably just before his family's move from Dockwray Square to Ayton House, a fourth Wooden Dolly was put on the spot — but this one was not an original ship's figurehead, nor was it even in the likeness of a figurehead. Carved to coincide with the Coronation of King Edward VII, it represented an elderly fishwife with a fish basket on her back. That was the Dolly in place when Stan left the town, and which was still in place during my own early boyhood years in North Shields.[2]

At other times, Stan's letters were full of sheer joyous, nostalgic references to his time in North Shields.

My Dear ...

Got a hell of a kick out of your letter of the 6th. inst. enjoyed every line, reliving those wonderful care-free days with your vivid description, sprinkled with laughter & Tyneside humour.

I do'nt remember going to King St. school, I first started at a kindergarten at some house in Dockwray Square, it was down in a basement, then went to a private school in Tynemouth, it was called Gordon's — he was quite a character, he collected Cats, do'nt think he ever let them out of the house — you could smell the joint from Jarrow, the fish quay was like a garden of roses compared. The old screwball used to write poetry & we had to sit and listen to it all day long, his favourite one was "Ode to the Tyneside"— used to add new verses to it every day & ask our opinion. I once told him I did'nt like it & had to stand in the corner for an hour. Having so many cats I often wondered if he wrote "Kitten on the Keys"!

After this episode I was sent to a boarding school in Tynemouth I believe it was called Tynemouth College, the reason my folks had me board there was due to my always being in mischief & trouble at home, like setting fire to the house, (accidently of course) & falling into a barrel of fish guts in my best Sunday suit on the fish quay near the "Wooden Dolly," drinking Gin (thought it was water) got cockeyed & many more escapades too numerous to mention. Think this was the forerunner of my film character!

Got a terrific laugh out of your Dr. & Geordie gag — so typical. Reminded me of another similar gag about a coal miner who had terrible bow legs, his wife begged him to have an operation & have them straightened out, his excuse was "No hinney they're good enough to go to work in."[3]

I remember all the names you mention, especially Doyle & Gibson (Tommy & Albert) & the Armstrong Bros (John & Ginger) I was in Levy & Cardwell's Pantos with them (1906 & 7.) also Graham & Baron (Jack & Benny) Georgie Wood etc. Knew Billy Mould when he had the Palace Of Varieties when my Dad ran the old Theatre Royal & the "Boro" also Wallsend — Jarrow — Hebburn & Blyth. Did you know Adam Tomlinson he was a funny comic, he used to have a shoe store in N.S. Len Long was another comic I used to enjoy, he's still living in South Shields, came to see me when I played Newcastle in '53. I think if we met we could talk for hours on end, Even tho' I was born in Lancashire, I've always felt I belong to Shields, I was very fond of Horace Lee, used to call him Uncle Horace — a sweet guy. I had the pleasure of seeing him again in '32. It was quite an emotional meeting, both cried like kids.

Thought I'd die re the 'apenny Dips & Black Bullets etc. what a memory you have.[4]

Due to my recent illness I have'nt been doing much of late — just resting & taking things easy till I'm fit & able again — have four Feature films to make as soon as I get in shape to work, so please do'nt hesitate in writing me any time, I enjoy very much corresponding with you.

I never heard of the guy you mention, Raynor Lehr, he probably was an Extra in some Western Movies — the San Fernando Valley is full of these characters.

I got a big laugh re your Mother beating up Tichey Lynn in front of the class — what a scream that must have been,

Well, all for now, ... it was nice to hear from you again, I got a lot of pleasure reminiscing with you.

Bye now, good luck & God Bless.

Sincerely: —

Stan.

137

Dear ...

Sorry so long in acknowledging your nice letter of June 1st. As you know we have been busy moving and have'nt had time for correspondence. We found a nice apartment here, a brand new building & right on the beach (sands).[5] We have been here now two weeks & I like it very much, think living by the ocean will do us both a lot of good. The apt. is newly furnished & so much easier for Eda to take care of.[6]

Just had a letter from Georgie Wood. he's been quite ill & in hospital, but says he [is] back home again & feeling much better.

Pleased to know you are having such nice weather, hope you will get a good share of it this year. Your mention of the Electric train rides to Tynemouth for a 1d return, bring back many happy memories, I [re]member I used to go to school in Tynemouth & ride the old steam train every day, that was quite an event for me to go by myself with my school bag strapped on my back — wearing knickers & cap! Sometimes I had to walk. I spent my fare on mint Black Bullets!, they used to sell big ones at a penny apiece — I asked the lady in the shop once, how long she would let me have for a H'appney, as I only had that much & she would'nt cut one in half— anyway she gave me one on the promise to pay the rest later![7]

Bye ... dear, take care of yourself & God Bless.

Sincerely:—

Stan Laurel.

xxx

Eda joins in love & kind thoughts.

It is obvious from some of his letters that Stan was not just indulging in nostalgia when writing about North Shields. He knew what was happening in the town as these examples from 1957 to 1959 so amply illustrate:

Dear ...

Many thanks your very interesting letter 9th.inst. with enclosure of the clipping regarding the new "Wooden Dolly." A friend of mine just sent me some post card pictures of the new Tyne Tunnel. Its certainly a wonderful project — I told my friend, he would have to wear his Sunday clothes every-time he went through it, its too nice to gen through in yer bare feet![8]

It looks like they are really modernizing the old Tyneside, I would'nt be surprised if the new "Wooden Dolly" looks like Marilyn Monroe, they'll probably have a water tank in her Creel to keep live Silver Herring!. I imagine the old "H'appney Dodger" (Tyne Ferry) will be going out of business & one of the discarded Navy Battleships will be used instead.[9]

... It was very interesting indeed to read your letter that appeared in the *Evening Chronicle*, bequeathing your eyes & Bodies to go to the R.V.I. & Medical school, that was certainly a wonderful gesture. Over here, people are paid for this, hospitals will buy your body in advance & after a death will have claim on it for research — I think I'd get about Fourpence Three Farthings for mine, think I'll wait till prices go up!! I'm at least worth a Bob!

Well, think I'll be gaan hinney, thanks again for your kind thoughts & wishes — enjoyed hearing from you again.[10]

My kind regards & best to Mr __ & self, trust alls well & happy.

Bye, good luck & God Bless.

Sincerely always,

Stan Laurel.

My Dear ...

Thank you for the lovely remembrance — very sweet of you.

Hope you had a lovely Xmas & the New Year will bring you lots of good health & happiness.

I had quite a few letters & cards from my friends on the Tyneside, you all made my Xmas very happy, wish I could fully express the pleasure it gave me, bless your hearts.

I understand great changes are being made in N. Shields. Dockwray Square where I used to live is all being torn down to make way for new flats, the old "Boro" theater that my Dad originally built has closed for good, & they are going to have a brand new "Wooden Dolly," they are sure fixing up the old Town, all the old land marks are gradually disappearing — everybody will soon have to wear their Sunday clothes every day.

Weather here is very warm — like summer, 84 degrees today, the only snow we see here is on Television!

Well, all for now, trust alls well & happy.

Good luck & God Bless you.

Sincerely always:

Stan Laurel.

My Dear ...

... Note you have been having unusually cold weather this year, must have put the ice cream people out of business! They are having a great deal of snow in the Eastern States right now — how lucky I am to be in So. California.

I was shocked when I heard about that terrible plane crash with the Manchester United Football Team aboard — what a tragedy, all young lads.[11]

I enjoyed reading the items you enclosed — very interesting. Well I'll have to be a gaan now, dinner's ready — am having a Tyneside Pheasant (a kipper with a feather stuck in it.!!!).[12]

Bye, good luck & God Bless.

Sincerely always:

Dear ...

... Interesting to hear that Marden has now developed into a Town, they are certainly making great progress in modernizing "Canny Aad Shields," I can imagine the changes that have been made since I last visited there — even to a new 'Wooden Dolly' in Northumberland Square.[13]

... Its a bit early yet, but I take this opportunity to wish you a very Merry Xmas & a Happy New Year, lots of good health & happiness always.

Take care of yourself "Hinney"

Sincerely always:

PS. Enclosed some stamps for your friend

Dear ...

Thanks for your welcome letter,15th.inst.

Glad you are enjoying the nice weather & feeling good. Too bad there is so much unemployment — it must be very discouraging to all these people — I guess if the Shipyards are not doing any business, there's nothing can be done about it. Lets hope conditions will improve & get the men back on the job again.

I had a letter from Jack Hogg, said there was a newspaper strike going on there — you probably know about it.

Eda & I are feeling pretty good dear, so everything is fine with us.

Yes the Television has done a lot of harm to the Theatre business & many of the Cinemas too, they can't compete with free entertainment, & its more convenient for people to stay at home & see a show in comfort, in bad weather especially.

I heard that the Empire in Sunderland had closed down — I was'nt surprised, they have'nt done good business for a long time now, did'nt think it would last as long as it did in fact.

Not much to tell you dear, so all for now.

Love & fond thoughts from us both here, to Dorothy self & her Hubby. Take care of yourself dear.

God Bless.

As ever:

Stan Laurel.

xxx xxx

On other occasions, Stan waxed lyrical about things just a little further afield than North Shields — in Blyth, for example, where his father had rebuilt the local Theatre Royal. In a 1957 letter he wrote:

.... I remember the old theater that was on the same site which my Dad was running, it was a very run down affair — benches instead of chairs, sawdust on the floors, cement stairs to the gallery, gas was the only lighting it had, it used to play old time melodramas & was nick-named "The Blood Tub." Anyway, it used to do a wonderful business & the place was always packed. My Dad felt very greatful to the people of Blyth for their generous support & thought it would be a nice gesture to show his appreciation by building a nice new modern theater for their pleasure & entertainment, he thought they deserved it in return for their wonderful patronage in the past.

Well, he invested a great deal of money & the New Theatre Royal was erected, the most modern theater of its time — electric lighting, the floors were carpeted, tip up red velvet chairs etc. Lifts instead of stairs to the Balcony & Gallery, even had a nursery with nurses in attendance to take care of the children so the parents & others in the audience would'nt be disturbed during the performance. The orchestra were in evening dress, the Stage crew in white uniforms, also the program & chocolate boys dressed as page boys with white gloves — not a thing was spared. Believe it or not it turned out a fiasco, the place was to elegant & the people would'nt come in, they liked the sawdust & wooden benches much better, they felt out of place in the beautiful surroundings, I imagine the feeling was they would have to be dressed up instead of coming in their weekday clothes, so the only time they did come was Saturday night, wearing their Sunday suit!. It broke my Dad financially so he gave it up along with his other Theatre — was'nt that awful? Yes, I have a memory of Blyth I shall never forget.

... hope I did'nt bore you with the story of the Blyth incident, but I thought it would be interesting to you.

My kind regards to ... & yourself, trust alls well & happy.

Bye now, good luck & God Bless.

Stan Laurel.

In 1959, he commented in another letter on the plans for his father's Theatre Royal:

Dear ...

Many thanks for your interesting letter with enclosure of news clippings re the Old Theatre Royal, Blyth, & the news letter of Bert Cole a former employee in the early days, it was indeed in those days a beautiful theatre, complete in every detail a credit to any community. I hope it will be considered & converted into a Civic Auditorium, & will be spared destruction — I feel the building has historic value as a landmark & should be preserved — The Town & district need such a place to hold their local meeting & important affairs, besides establishing talent & local Culture in the future.

Stan not only corresponded with people from back home. They also came to stay with him in California.

Dear ...

...We have some friends visiting here from England, we went to school together in 1900 & have corresponded for many years, we are having a wonderful time reminiscing our early days, you can imagine we have plenty to talk about. They left England last September & toured South Africa & Australia, they leave next week for a trip to Canada & will sail home in May from Montreal.

He was a Concert pianist & entertainer but now retired, they have a lovely home near Newcastle-On-Tyne, Eng. but they love to travel to various Countries, so they really enjoy life.

Think thats all for now, so Eda joins in love & best to you both.

Our kind thoughts always:

As Stan grew up in a fishing port, it is not surprising that he retained a love of the sea and fishing all his life. In his prime, he loved being at sea and fishing and in retirement opted for apartments first in Santa Monica and then Malibu, with views of the Pacific.[13] Shortly after Stan's 65th birthday and when still recuperating from a stroke, an American correspondent suggested he would enjoy living in Apple Valley, California. Stan replied: "I know Apple Valley is a wonderful spot, but for some reason the Desert & Mountains are very depressing to me — am much happier near the Beach & Ocean — should have been a sailor I guess!" As he explained in a 1959 letter, he loved to go fishing in the boat he owned.

My only regret is, I am not able to continue my favourite sport, Sword Fishing. Due to the after effects of my slight stroke I suffered in '55. Am not to active anymore, its too strenuous for me. I was a Gold Button member of the Avalon Tuna Club at Catalina Island for several years — had a nice 45 ft. boat fully equipped for fishing, twin Hall-Scott motors (275 H.P. each) with a speed of 22 knots. During World War II, the Navy took over Island (Catalina) for a training station, so no private craft was allowed in those waters, so I decided to get rid of it — no sense in letting it rot in Dry Dock.

Stan's final home was modest but, as he explained to one of his correspondents, it was all he and his wife needed and had the advantage of being very close to the sea.

Dear ...

Thank you for your nice letter of May 20th.ult. Sorry I took so long to acknowledge, reason is I rented our house in Santa Monica, the place was too large & a lot of hard work for Mrs Laurel to take care of now that I am unable to help her, so we decided to move into a smaller place to make things easier for her. The house had seven big rooms & two bath rooms, so you can imagine all the cleaning to be done — 24 windows with venetian blinds — it was really a big-job, lawns & gardens had to be kept up too, all unnecessary for just two people. However, we found a very nice little Apartment here in Malibu, a brand new building right on the beach (sands) only about 40 feet from the water, the front balcony overlooks the ocean. Mrs L. likes to swim, so the place is ideal for us, only one big living room with built in kitchen, one bedroom & bath — all we need & very modern. Its a nice section & just a short distance from the famous Malibu Movie Colony, all the well known Stars have homes there, they are small estates with private beaches, we are very fortunate in finding such a beautiful spot, so I think we shall enjoy the change very much & I think the sea air will do us both a lot of good. We get about 8 months summer here & the winters are very mild — just a rainy season — no snow. We rented our house unfurnished so it was quite a job moving everything into storage. However it was worth all the trouble.

Stan, of course, did more than correspond with friends about North Shields. When the opportunity arose, he revisited the town — the town to which he said he felt he belonged. He was to return in triumph on his first visit in 1932 although the visit did not turn out as he had originally hoped. He discovered to his cost that being Stan Laurel no longer allowed him to be Stan Jefferson, not even for a single day. His later visits to Tyneside in 1947, 1952 and 1953 were to prove mixed experiences. When he left to return to the United States for the final time in 1953, it was as a tired old trouper, with his wonderful career behind him.

8

Returns to the "Old Town"

Stan left North Shields with his family in 1905, at the age of 15. He returned with the Levy Cardwell Pantomime Company in *The Sleeping Beauty* at the Theatre Royal for a week beginning March 30, 1908, when he was 17. However, there are no further recorded visits to the town until 1932, when he was 42.

In the 24 years between, the fortunes of North Shields had changed considerably. The people he had left behind had suffered first from the hideous "war to end all wars" from 1914 to 1918. As many as 6.2 million UK citizens were mobilized (until 1916, all of them volunteers)—almost 14 percent of a population of 46 million. The scale of the casualties, and lasting impact of the war on the families affected, is difficult to comprehend. Almost one million UK citizens were killed and a further 1.7 million wounded (almost 6 percent of the population). In comparison, 117,000 U.S. citizens were killed and 206,000 injured—0.35 percent of a population of 92 million.

The First World War was followed by a massive economic slump as the world's nations struggled to return to a peace-time economy. Matters in the UK were made worse by deteriorating industrial relations, including a divisive general strike in 1926. Subsequently, following the Wall Street stock market crash of 1929, the global economy spiraled into a deep depression to which no one appeared to have an answer. Wages fell, unemployment rose and those without work became subject to the indignities of the household means test. At this stage, the vast majority of people in North Shields still lived without what are now considered the minimum basics of a plumbed hot water supply, indoor toilet and bathroom. Life was even worse for the thousands who still lived in the riverside and bankside slums which, far from being the homes "fit for heroes" promised by the 1919 Housing Act, were soon to be declared unfit for human habitation as the 1930 Housing Act came into effect.[1]

1932: A "High" for Stan During a "Low" for Shields

Life had been much better for Stan Laurel. Although he had lost $30,000 in the stock market crash of 1929 (the equivalent of over $4 million in 2008, measured in terms of relative share of GDP), the continued success of the Laurel and Hardy films meant that his personal future was secure (McCabe, 1976, p. 149). After many long and tiring years at the Roach Studio, Stan decided that he needed a complete break. He decided on a holiday in England. Oliver Hardy, who also had roots in England, decided he would like to accompany him. Initially, they seem to have thought of it as a social trip. They would visit friends and family, see the sights, play golf and go fishing. MGM, the distributor of their films, had other ideas. They drew up a travel plan and organized it around a big publicity campaign. Thanks to some meticulous research by A.J. Marriot, the details of this and their other UK tours have been well documented (Marriot, 1993). It has only been necessary for me to complement his work with additional local material relating to their visits to North Shields.

At this stage in their careers, Stan and Babe (as Stan often referred to Oliver Hardy in public as well as private) may not have been aware what a huge following they had in Britain. Making shorts to support the main feature films, which is all they were doing at this stage, did not put them amongst the biggest stars in the Hollywood firmament. Yet they arrived at Southampton in July 1932 to a tumultuous welcome. Thousands of fans were waving, cheering and whistling the Laurel and Hardy signature tune "The Cuckoo Song." They were greeted with similar scenes when they reached London. The crowds put them under such pressure that Stan and Babe became separated and only met up again later at the Savoy Hotel. By the end of the day, Stan and Babe could have had no doubt about the scale of their public following. They went to see Noël Coward's play *Cavalcade* at the Drury Lane Theatre and received a standing ovation from a packed house as they took their seats in a box. Afterwards they were invited backstage for a private party with the great man, then at the height of his theatrical success.

From then on, they were mobbed wherever they went. After several days of dodging London crowds while making public appearances, they caught the overnight sleeper to Newcastle upon Tyne on July 27. Their visit was hardly a secret. The *Shields Daily News* had carried as its headline story:

VISIT OF FAMOUS FILM STARS TO NORTH SHIELDS
LAUREL AND HARDY
HERE TOMORROW

By the time they arrived in Newcastle and a car drove them the eight miles to the Grand Hotel, Tynemouth on the coast, where they were to spend the night, it was still early morning. Ahead of them lay a long day in a town in the depths of the Depression with a population desperately in need of something to lift it from the misery of everyday life.

Britain as a whole was in a deep depression in 1932 but the northeast of England was particularly hard-hit. Preston Colliery, the last coal mine to be worked in North Shields, had closed in 1928 with the loss of over 1,000 jobs. The number of unemployed in the town fluctuated between 4,500 and 7,500 at a time when the total population of the Borough (including children) was about 65,000. Many more were under-employed and even those in work had by then been obliged to accept a series of wage cuts in an ill-judged attempt to ameliorate the country's economic problems. At a time when there was usually only one breadwinner in a family, it meant that a much larger number of people were subsisting at or below the poverty level. When the limited unemployment insurance benefit ran out, the unemployed and their families were subject to the humiliation of the hated "household means test" introduced in November 1931. Benefit was paid only after a meticulous investigation of a household's "means," conducted to ensure that its members had no undisclosed earnings, savings, or other means of support. Attempts to bring new industries into the town were conspicuously unsuccessful and not helped by a government policy which favored workers moving to places where work was available.

Little of this would have been immediately obvious to Stan and Oliver as visitors to the town, especially when they arrived not in North Shields itself but in nearby Tynemouth. It was still very much a pretty coastal village and, though it may have owed its comfortable elegance to the soot and grime generated in North Shields, it had never been spoiled by industry itself.

Even though they arrived early in the morning, members of the press were there to greet them. Stan told the *Shields Daily News* reporter that he was glad to have a chance of a return visit to North Shields because he had so many memories of the town. His only regret was that their tight schedule meant that they would not be able to stroll around the landmarks he knew as a boy (*Shields Daily News*, July 28, 1932).

After a few hours sleep, Stan and Oliver were at breakfast in the Grand Hotel with Eileen Jefferson, the daughter of Stan's brother Gordon, who had come down from Newcastle to meet them. The mayor and mayoress of Tynemouth then arrived to escort them to North Shields Town Hall, which was just a couple of minutes walk from Stan's original Dockwray Square home. On its arrival, the car was surrounded by a large crowd (held back by a police cordon), determined to get a good look at the local hero. Stan and Oliver emerged from the car to a tremendous burst of cheering.

The reception in the mayor's parlor included local dignitaries and the inevitable representatives of the press, plus many of the people whom Stan had known as a boy. Whether or not he had time to do any more than say hello to them I do not know. After cocktails, they crossed the road to the Albion Assembly Rooms for lunch. On the way, they were again mobbed, despite a strong police presence. Even during lunch they were not able to put aside their celebrity personas. They were inundated with requests for autographs but both men appear to have taken this constant intrusive attention in good spirits.

Stan spoke first in reply to the mayor's toast. In his usual quiet, unassuming manner he said, "Mr Mayor, aldermen, councillors, and old pals, I do not know what to say for the marvellous reception. I was not born in North Shields, but I feel that I just belong here. I am proud to be amongst you all. I owe a lot to Mr. Hardy for making it possible for me to be in this position to come here and enjoy your wonderful reception. I feel I want to thank everybody personally. God bless you all."

Oliver Hardy, the stranger in town, was full of praise for his hosts when he stood up to say his few words. In other places, at other times, his words might have seemed "over the top." But this was North Shields. He was meeting Geordies for the first time: people renowned for their openness and warmth. And the year was 1932, a time of deep economic recession. The five cinemas in the town provided the main form of escape from an unhappy world. In all, they had a staggering 6,644 seats; offered two or three shows daily and a change of program twice a week.[2] So for anyone "from the pictures" to visit North Shields would have been a major event. But for two stars whose own 1931 film *Come Clean* was showing at the Prince's Theatre that very week — stars who could make you laugh at a time when you wanted to cry — to come all the way from Hollywood to see you when you were struggling just to make ends meet, must have meant a very great deal to the canny folks of Shields. Their overwhelming gratitude would have expressed itself in the warmth of their welcome to their own Stan and his unassuming partner Ollie. Oliver, it must also be remembered, loved observing people and had a genuine interest in them. His wife once said of him that "he loved people; in a way, people were his hobby" and a former colleague emphasized how genuine he was and that there was never anything phony about him (McCabe, 1976, pp. 79, 90). So there can be little doubt that what Oliver Hardy had to say on that day was the result of his being genuinely moved:

> Mrs. Hardy and I want to stay here forever. You have accepted us and made us feel at home. From the bottom of my heart, I wish to thank you. I have never in all my life met with such hearty people, such kindly people, such courteous people, or such considerate people.

Oliver appears to have confided to a reporter that he anticipated that during the civic reception Stan would be given the "Freedom of the City" (or, more precisely in the case of Tynemouth, the "Freedom of the Borough"). We will never know whether his remark was based on pure surmise or whether someone had given him or Stan some intimation that such an honor was about to be conferred on him. What we do know is that no such honor was afforded Stan Laurel and, if it had been, it would have been an unparalleled event. During its 124-year history, Tynemouth offered the Freedom of the Borough to only eight individuals, all of whom were former mayors.[3] Many other towns and cities have made use of the honor as a way of acknowledging their respect for former residents who have distinguished themselves in some way (e.g., when Liverpool honored the Beatles); for esteemed visitors (e.g., when Hull honored South Africa's Archbishop Desmond Tutu) or for newcomers who have made an outstanding contribution to the town (e.g., when Derby honored soccer manager Brian Clough). In Tynemouth, its civic leaders chose instead to limit the honor to their own number.

At some point during the afternoon, Stan slipped out of the reception, hoping to spend some time alone in Dockwray Square, the place that had meant so much to him as a boy. He failed in that most modest of aspirations. As a celebrity, he now had to endure the price of fame. A large crowd, anticipating that he would visit Dockwray Square, had already gathered there hoping to get a closer look at the local boy made good. Stan did manage to get near to number 8, but getting inside was out of the question. Had he succeeded, he would have found it very different from the up-market, single-occupancy dwelling he had known in his boyhood. The electoral register for the period recorded six separate households at number 8, comprising 11 adults. In addition, there would probably have been children living there and possibly other adults who were not on the electoral register.

Nevertheless, even though his visit to Dockwray Square may not have been all that he wanted, he was later to say of his boyhood home, "It is a place for sentiment with me. I belong to Dockwray Square."

Having been picked up by the police escort which had fought through the crowd to reach him, Stan was driven about half a mile to where his second home Ayton House had been. It is not clear what was left of the original house by this time. The *Shields Daily News* of June 12, 1931, following an interview with Horace Lee, the former manager of the Theatre Royal, reported that Ayton House has been pulled down some years earlier. According to the electoral registers it had by then been empty for some time and the Council minutes of the period contain many references to it over a period of years, as negotiations were conducted with several parties to try to find an alternative use for the house and site.

Stan and Oliver, who after a night with very little sleep must have been exhausted, were next returned to the Grand Hotel where they arrived not to peace and quiet, but to re-join the mayoral party which had been driven down to the coast while Stan had been trying unsuccessfully to

Stan clowning on the steps outside his former home, 8 Dockwray Square, during his visit to North Shields in 1932. In his boyhood, the Jeffersons had occupied the whole house. In 1932, it was occupied by six separate households. The photograph was taken by Stan's boyhood friend Roland Park, who had a well-known photographic business in North Shields. (Courtesy of Roland Craig [grandson of the photographer Roland Park].)

have some quality time in his boyhood haunts. Right on schedule at 3 pm, Laurel, Hardy and their entourage walked from the hotel to the huge Plaza Palace, which then towered over Tynemouth's "Long Sands."[4] As soon as Stan emerged from the hotel, he was mobbed again. It seemed as if everyone wanted to touch, kiss or shake hands with him. The VIPs then took their places on the terrace at the rear of the Plaza, facing the beach and sea where they could be seen by the thousands of spectators. Many, of course, would have been there on the beach whether or not Laurel and Hardy were in town. This was a July day during the summer holidays and people from much further afield than North Shields and Tynemouth would have been enjoying a day at the seaside. Very few families at that time would have been in a position to go away on holiday.

The Grand Hotel, Tynemouth, where Stan and Oliver stayed overnight in 1932 and for two weeks in 1952. (Courtesy of Nigel Hastie of the Grand Hotel, Tynemouth.)

Film of the event shows that throughout the proceedings Laurel and Hardy switched between their screen roles (effortlessly improvising gags at each stage) and being their warm human selves. After the welcomes were over, this time it was Hardy who was first to speak. He finished by promising: "I will be down amongst you all soon." When Stan stood up, he allowed himself to be kissed, hugged and patted on the back, and had his hand shaken until it must have hurt. He signed autographs and posed for photographs with as many people as time allowed. Then, when there was no sign of the queue ever coming to an end, he turned to the crowd and said: "I love you all. I would like to shake hands with you all and say thank you. It is the greatest day of my life. I shall always remember this visit to Tynemouth." Then, obviously choked with emotion, he sat down and wiped away real tears. Oliver could do nothing to console him. Later, Stan wrote to the editor of the *Shields Hustler*, "What a great homecoming

The view of the Plaza and Long Sands from the Grand Hotel in the early 1930s, as it would have looked during Laurel and Hardy's visit in 1932 when they appeared at the rear of the Plaza overlooking the crowded beach below. (North Tyneside Local Studies Library.)

it was! I shall never forget it as long as I live. I had a lump in my throat the whole time" (*Shields Hustler* 5, 1932).

The crowd watching from the beach and the terraces and staircases of the Plaza were then joined by 600 underprivileged children who had been able to come thanks to a recently established charity, the Sunshine Fund.[5] Stan and Oliver presented the donated gifts to all 600 of them. Despite their tiredness, they continued to smile and play-act throughout this mammoth task with warmth and good grace. Stan even joined in the line of children at one stage and tried to get Oliver to give him a present only to be rewarded with the same impatient "short shrift" he would have received on screen. Silent footage of the occasion is available on VHS video and a low compression version (with an Italian commentary) can be viewed on YouTube.

Their long day was not yet over. At 9 pm they made an appearance at the Queen's Hall in Newcastle, which was followed by a visit to the Stoll Picture House (another former theater). Stan also met up with Horace Lee, a former manager of the Theatre Royal in North Shields.

After meeting Stan, a reporter from the *Shields Hustler* wrote:

> What struck us all was Stan's sweet naturalness. Success hasn't spoilt him, as it does so many people. He has not developed a swelled head, and his old friends in North Shields were glad of that. There is something sad to witness men who have succeeded in forgetting themselves, and putting on airs — airs that invariably do not become them. Stan is "being himself" and we like him all the better for it [Marriot, 1993, p. 55].

After breakfast the following morning, barely 24 hours after having arrived on Tyneside, Stan and Oliver were on their way again. While waiting for the train at Newcastle Central Station to take them to Scotland, Stan left the following message for the people of Tyneside: "God bless everybody. I love them all. Tyneside people do not alter, they are as good as ever."

From Scotland, Laurel and Hardy visited Blackpool, Manchester, Sheffield and Birmingham before they returned to London. Everywhere they went, they were greeted by thousands of adoring fans. Two days later, they were on their way to Paris. Hardy volunteered, "We shall stay in Paris for ten days and hide from everyone." That proved to be wishful thinking. The president of France sent his car and they were driven down the Champs Elysées as if national heroes; Claridge's informed the press that they were being treated as honored guests (i.e., staying free of charge) and from then on they could find no peace. Now knowing what to expect, they reluctantly cancelled their planned sightseeing tour of Deauville, Berlin, Antwerp, Brussels and Madrid and returned to London. There they did at least manage a few days respite from their fans before returning to the U.S. on August 24.

Although it had been an exhausting visit and perhaps very different from what Stan had original anticipated, he did appreciate the overwhelmingly warm reception that he and Oliver Hardy had received. As he recalled in a letter to a friend in England: "I sure did have a wonderful reception at home didn't I? It all seems like a dream — everybody treated us royally. I'll never forget it as long as I live. God bless them all."

1947: After the War—A Warm Welcome in a Cold Country

Between 1927 and 1940, Laurel and Hardy's career at the Hal Roach Studio was phenomenally successful. However, although their subsequent films for Twentieth Century–Fox and MGM were moneymakers, they had not provided them with a sufficient sense of achievement to accept the offer made in 1945 to renew their contracts for a further five years. They chose to seek new pastures. The options were limited. Television was still in its infancy. They had enjoyed considerable success in theatrical productions since leaving Roach but vaudeville was fast disappearing.

Fortuitously, they were then offered a 12-week engagement in British theaters by impresario Bernard Delfont. This time (1947) they arrived in the UK not in mid-summer but in February. Britain was then going through a period of prolonged austerity. With the help of her American ally she may have won the war against the Fascist regimes of Germany and Italy but, in the process, had gone from being the world's largest creditor to being the world's largest debtor. The period of postwar reconstruction, just begun, was proving very painful. Nature too was being unusually unkind. From January to March, Britain experienced record low temperatures and heavy and persistent falls of snow. Fuel was short and life was hard. *Enter left, Laurel and Hardy*, and things began to look just a little brighter for those lucky enough to get tickets for their shows.

As A.J. Marriot's research shows, they were greeted at Southampton by a scene comparable to that which they had enjoyed in 1932. Once more they caught the train to London where, with thousands of fans crowding in to see them, they again became separated, just as they had been 15 years earlier. Unnerved by the crush, Oliver sought refuge on a bus. When the surprised driver asked him where he wanted to go, he said, "Anywhere as long as it's away from here," and then added, "and on to the Savoy" (Marriot, 1993, p. 85).

The next morning, they were to get their first taste of postwar reconstruction Britain. With so many commodities still rationed (even bread which had been freely available during the war had been rationed since 1946), Laurel and Hardy had to queue like everyone else for their ration books. As a photograph taken at the time shows, they registered by candlelight because the combination of bad weather and fuel shortages made power cuts far from unusual.

After rehearsing their act in London, they set off to open their tour in Newcastle. Apparently Oliver was apprehensive at the prospect of his first appearance in a British theater, the Moss Empire on Newgate Street.[6] He need not have been concerned. The theater was packed and Laurel and Hardy's act was well received. What *was* a cause for anxiety was the worsening weather. As Stan remarked to the reporters who had been invited to a party at the Royal Station Hotel, "Last time we came to England in 1932 it was the hottest summer you had ever had. Now look at it. It's the worst winter you've had for years" (*The Evening News*, February 24, 1947). In fact, it was the worst winter Britain had experienced since 1814!

By now snow had blocked most major roads, and smaller roads were impassable. The London and North Eastern Railway line was also completely blocked. Coal, already in short supply, had become an even more precious commodity because colliery workers were unable to get to work. At night, the temperature plummeted to as low as 8.6°F. In contrast, when Oliver phoned his wife Lucille, he learned that the temperature in California was 80.6°F. He went back to Stan and Ida's hotel room that night and found them huddled around a small coal fire. When he told them that Lucille was basking in sunshine, Stan picked up the last piece of coal, threw it on the fire and declared, "Ah well, there'll always be an England." With that remark they "broke up" and laughed "until the tears cascaded down their cheeks" (Marriot, 1993, p. 87). To understand their mirth, readers must appreciate that during the Second World War "There'll Always Be an England" was an immensely popular, morale-boosting song, written (music by Ross Parker and Harry Par-Davies, lyrics by Hugh Charles) when Britain was anticipating an imminent invasion by Nazi troops. It had been recorded by the biggest UK recording star of the period, Vera Lynn, and also sung by Deanna Durbin as the culminating scene in the Universal film *Nice Girl?*[7]

On February 26, the Wednesday of their week's run in Newcastle, Laurel and Hardy returned to North Shields for the first time since 1932. They chose a terrible day for their visit. That night's *Evening News* reported that a storm began "shortly after midnight and by 5 am a 45 mph north easterly gale was driving the snow hard before it." Some local roads were blocked for a time and between 7 am and 9 am there were no trains running between Newcastle and North Shields. Although the local newspaper described the overnight blizzards as the worst in living memory, leading to the 4,800-ton Greek ship *Zephyros* being driven onto the rocks at Cullercoats, Laurel and Hardy still visited the town as the weather eased. Naturally, the awful weather and its consequences dominated the front page of the *Shields Evening News* that night. Laurel and Hardy's visit was relegated to no more than a couple of column inches at the foot of the front page, though there was more coverage of the visit the following day.

North Shields was much changed since their visit 15 years earlier. The bankside by the river had been cleared of housing shortly after their 1932 visit and the program of building new suburban estates on the outskirts of the town, which had accompanied the clearance, was still continuing. On their last visit the town had been in the grip of a terrible depression when thousands of workers had been unemployed for long periods. By 1947, the country had returned to more or less "full" employment but was suffering in other ways. After six years of war, the town was still disfigured by numerous bomb sites. As actors who had played the role of air raid wardens on screen in MGM's wartime film *Air Raid Wardens* (1943), the horrors of what that role would have entailed in reality in North Shields would have been particularly sobering to Stan and Oliver. A Luftwaffe map of the period shows that Stan's former home in Dockwray Square was not far from the prime bombing targets which it had identified in North Shields. Moreover, one of the worst bombing incidents in the UK had taken place just a short distance from his Dockwray Square home. There can be no doubt that Stan would have learned of that particular tragedy and also been familiar with the onslaught of bombing to which his boyhood town had been subjected.

During the war, the warning sirens of impending bombing raids were sounded over 250 times in North Shields and, on each occasion, the people had to rush to the nearest air raid shelter. Although in the majority of cases the bombers flew over because they were targeting other locations in the area, official records show that at least 310 high explosive bombs were dropped on North Shields, along with 18,000 incendiary bombs and 19 parachute mines. They resulted in 447 properties being demolished or damaged beyond repair, and a further 9,928 damaged but judged reparable. Despite the provision of air raid shelters, 225 people died, 150 suffered serious injuries and a further 325 were slightly injured (*Evening News*, October 13, 1944).

The incident which caused the greatest loss of life at a single moment in time was only about 250 yards from Dockwray Square. At around midnight on May 3, 1941, a single high explosive bomb from a German aircraft hit Wilkinson's soft drinks factory at the junction of King and George Streets. Sheltering in the basement, under the heavy machinery, were people from the immediate vicinity. When the floor, walls, machinery and debris collapsed into the basement shelter, 96 of them were killed. Others died later in hospital from their injuries. The total death toll was 107. Of those, 41 were children under the age of 16.[8]

Stan was able to have a more relaxed visit to Dockwray Square in 1947 than had been possible in 1932. Then his hope of being able to indulge in a little quiet nostalgia had been thwarted by the crowds of fans. In 1947, with a week in which to choose his moment, he and Oliver found the Square relatively empty. As guests of the mayor, Frank Mavin, they arrived in his chauffeur-driven limousine. Oliver was later to say that Stan was so excited as he neared his old home that "he almost jumped out of the car." But, after inspecting the area, Stan confessed, "It's very distressing to see how the place has been knocked about during the war." Many years later, Mavin recalled that Stan was shocked and became very emotional at seeing Dockwray Square and his old home in such a bad state.[9]

Not all the changes he saw were the result of war. It is true that the iron railings had been cut down for scrap metal and that a gun emplacement and a barrage balloon anchored on Dockwray Square would have meant that the garden area would have been in bad shape. However, after almost 200 years, all the houses in Dockwray Square were beginning to show their age and the people who lived in them were no longer the town's notables.

The trend towards multi-occupation which was already in evidence when the Jeffersons lived there had continued. The electoral records for 1947 suggest that 8 Dockwray Square now housed at least eight households, comprising 12 adults and an unknown number of children. The houses were shabbier than they had been in Stan's day and the tenants of the rooms were now all ordinary folk.[10] If those ordinary folk looked tired and depressed during Stan's visit, it was hardly surprising. Like so many other people, all over Britain, after enduring the depression years of the 1930s and a brutal war from 1939 to 1945, they were now doing their best to cope with the war's painful aftermath. Postwar reconstruction, however necessary, compounded their problems. It meant continued rationing and general austerity, all made worse by the worst winter in decades. Food and fuel were in such short supply that residents could not even eat bread and margarine whenever they wanted, or be sure that they would have enough coal for their domestic coal fires.[11]

Stan and Oliver went to the Boro' which in Stan's boyhood days had been a theater (built by his father) but was now a cinema. They then went

The west side of Dockwray Square, North Shields, as it looked in 1947 around the time of Stan's visit. A few years later, after the multi-occupied houses were judged no longer fit for human habitation, it was decided to completely demolish the Square rather than refurbish the once elegant houses. The shoddily built apartment blocks which replaced them lasted not for 200 years but barely 20. (Courtesy of Stan Bewick and the Tynemouth Photographic Society and the North Tyneside Local Studies Library.)

The Arthur Jefferson Boro' Theatre was converted into a cinema in 1907 but badly damaged by fire in 1910. This is how it looked during Stan's last visit to the town in the 1950s. It subsequently closed and was demolished in the 1960s. (Courtesy of Stan Bewick and the Tynemouth Photographic Society.)

on to the empty site where the Theatre Royal had been before it was demolished in 1939: the place where his father had been the lessee, manager and performer, and in which Stan had spent so many happy hours as a child, developing his own passion to go on the stage. The visit ended with tea in the mayor's parlor and a civic reception at the Grand Hotel in Tynemouth.

From Newcastle, Stan and Oliver went on to make similar bill-topping appearances elsewhere. Their first stop was Birmingham where they were hoping for a predicted thaw in the awful weather. Instead, they had the heaviest snowfall of the winter so far, accompanied by gusts of wind up to 40 miles per hour which created enormous snow drifts.

The weather continued to worsen as they moved on to the London Palladium. There were blizzards, a hurricane and flooding. During the night of the thaw, the Thames rose nine feet. There was flooding in 30 counties and roads were impassable almost everywhere. Despite the weather, the crowds kept pouring into the Palladium and the Laurel and Hardy run was extended from two to three weeks. During a prolonged cold spell in 2010, 67 years later, an article in the *Daily Telegraph* recalled that horrendous winter. Amongst the noteworthy events it listed, it included the huge crowds outside a Trafalgar Square cinema where, despite the freezing weather and oceans of slush, people were desperate to get the autographs of Laurel and Hardy.

And so the tour went on — for almost a whole year. Stan and Oliver criss-crossed the country until November, when their initial spell in Britain culminated in an appearance in the Royal Variety Command Performance at the London Palladium.[12] After touring Europe, Oliver returned to America on January 15, 1948. Stan went back to England where he stayed until the 28th before following his partner back to the warmer climes of California.

Their return to the United States was not an especially happy one. Stan's father died in 1949. Then Stan was diagnosed with diabetes. While his condition was stabilized, he persuaded Oliver to go it alone for the first time in over 20 years.[13] Shortly afterwards, they were invited to France to make the film *Atoll K* discussed in Chapter 6. However, as I have already explained, it was a most unhappy experience. It was a very disappointed (as well as tired and unwell) pair of comic actors who returned to America in early 1951.[14]

Though their popularity had revived during their absence thanks to the release of their films on TV, and they received offers of stage and screen work at home and abroad, for one reason or another they all came to nothing. So, when Bernard Delfont offered them a second tour of British theaters in 1952, they were happy to accept.

1952: Stan's Final Visit to North Shields

There has been a suggestion that Laurel and Hardy were booked into first class theaters in their 1947 UK tour but second class theaters in 1952 and, worse still, third class theaters in their final 1953 tour (MacGillivray, 2008, p. 246). The evidence does not lend ready support to this assertion.

They played seven prestigious Moss Empire theaters in 1947 but 14 theaters on the Moss circuit in 1952 and 12 during their final tour.[15] It may be true that they played in small towns in 1952 and 1953 but that was also the case in 1947. Nevertheless, there are several good reasons why Laurel and Hardy may have judged the second and third tours to have been much less satisfactory than their first.

When they docked at Southampton in January 1952, their first impression might have been that this tour was not going to be the same success story as 1947. There were fans to greet them but not on the scale of either 1932 or 1947. However, as they had arrived on the coldest day in Britain for two years, that was hardly surprising.

This time, after a spell rehearsing in London, the tour opened in Peterborough. As they came into the station, an enthusiastic crowd was waiting for them and, over the two weeks they were there, the show broke all previous box office records. They then went on to a stint in Glasgow before returning to Tyneside. For some reason, they did not repeat the success they had enjoyed in Peterborough. Whereas they might have expected to have done particularly well on Tyneside, because of Stan's connections with the area, their week at Newcastle's Moss Empire must have been disappointing if not disheartening. Moreover, their lukewarm reception at the theater was made worse by the accommodation arranged for them in Tynemouth. The only compensation was the warmth of their reception in North Shields and the opportunity the week gave Stan to look up old friends.

In 1947, Stan and Oliver had stayed at the Royal Station Hotel in Newcastle but Marriot records that they were unable to obtain a reservation there in 1952. At a time when there were relatively few hotels in the Tyneside area, they were booked instead into the Grand Hotel at Tynemouth, where they had spent one night in 1932 and been received at a civic reception in 1947. While the Grand enjoyed a better setting than the Royal Station Hotel, because of its commanding views over the sea, that was where the favorable comparison ended in 1952. At the time, the Grand Hotel was going through a difficult period and did not live up to its name. After acknowledging the large waiting crowd of fans, Stan and Oliver climbed the steps, not into a genuinely grand hotel, but a shabby place that evidently depressed them from the outset. As Stan wrote to a friend later:

161

We spent a miserable two weeks [at the Grand Hotel]. The place was so dilapidated & run down & most uncomfortable — was happy to leave the place. I wouldn't have stayed there one night if we could have found other accommodation.[16]

On Sunday, March 16, Stan and Oliver made a guest appearance before a full-house, 1,400-strong audience at a charity concert at the Gaumont Cinema in North Shields. The cinema, which had not long reopened after refurbishment following bomb damage in 1941, was floodlit for the occasion.[17] While Stan and Oliver's contracts did not allow them to perform, they still found a way to entertain the audience. As the 27-year-old master of ceremonies, Eric Nicholson, described later:

I do not think any experience ever brought the drama, immense enchantment, and sheer exhilaration which I felt that night. During one of my long rambling stories, the laughs were coming along nicely, and getting stronger by the second. I was thrilled. Great guffaws were greeting me, and at the end of the story there was rapturous applause. Just then, I saw two very good reasons for all the laughter and applause. There, walking towards me down the centre aisle were Stan Laurel and Oliver Hardy. The audience was going spare. What was I to do? There was I, a nobody, and bearing down on me were the world's two greatest comedians. The great men were now just a few rows away, and the audience were "tearing the place apart." Two spotlights hit them, and I blurted out, "Just you two wait till I get you up here." They stopped advancing, paused, then Ollie slowly put his hand up to his bowler hat and wiggled it. His hand descended to his tie which he pulled out and wiggled in turn. Stan's reaction to my "telling them off" was to burst into tears. At this, I, along with the audience, collapsed in total hysteria.

The furore lasted a full five minutes during which they ascended to the stage. The show was now well and truly stopped, and the two stars spent many minutes apologizing to me for interrupting my act. I needed no apologies at all. They'd made me that night. I was in ecstasy [Nicholson interviewed by A.J. Marriot, 1993, p. 171].

On stage, Stan and Oliver — accompanied by their wives — were given a civic welcome by the mayor of Tynemouth, Tommy Hails, who owned a fish and chip shop just a few yards from the site of the Theatre Royal. Oliver spoke first and introduced Stan to the audience: "This is going to be Stan's night ... Your boy and my boy, Stan Laurel!" Stan replied "It will be kinda difficult for me to express my, and our, grateful thanks ... it really is wonderful to be back in my home town."

He went on tell the audience about some of his memories of his time in North Shields including the occasion when he fell into a barrel of fish guts and had to be hosed down, and the time when, dressed in his best Eton suit for a birthday party, he was hit by a soot bomb.

> Then to the wild cheering and clapping of fourteen hundred people, the local-boy-made-good made his way to the circle, to watch the rest of the show [*Shields Evening News*, March 17, 1952].[18]

Before returning to the Grand Hotel, Stan and Oliver presented merit stars to two of the Gaumont's staff and signed innumerable autographs. On noting how happy and smiling the two comedians remained under this crowd of autograph hunters, a reporter asked Hardy, "Don't you get sick of this continual signing of autographs?" Without hesitation, he replied, "I'd get more sick if they didn't ask." On March 22, the *Shields Evening News* later reported, "Simple and sincere are this comedy pair. For politeness they take top marks. Autograph books were showered on them. Yet never a cross word — just a smile and a pleasant word."

The following evening Laurel and Hardy returned to the tour proper and began a week's engagement at the Newcastle Empire. They did not play to record full houses as they had done in Peterborough. On the contrary, during most performances the theater was only half full. As an usherette later recalled, "We would move the ones at the back to the seats near the front, so that from the stage it appeared full" (Marriot, 1993, p. 173).

Although the size of the audiences at the Empire must have been disappointing, Stan had other experiences during his visit to Tyneside which he found heart-warming and rewarding. Compared to his previous two return visits, it was easier for him to spend time with old friends. For example, he visited his boyhood pal Roland Park, who was a photographer with a shop in North Shields. He also sought out William Henry Harmon, who had worked for his father at the Theatre Royal.[19] As Stan's black saloon pulled up outside Harmon's modest terraced flat at 71 West Percy Street, Stan was treated to a big cheer from the neighbors. Once inside, Stan was told he hadn't changed a bit. Alas, Stan could not say the same of the gaunt Harmon, who had been an invalid for several years. But Stan appears to have handled that with his characteristic grace and wit: "How old are you?" asked Stan. "Seventy-two," replied Harmon. "Then I'll race you down the street!" said Stan. When asked about Ollie, Stan said, "The fog has made him lose his voice a bit." Then he laughed, "He's not a Geordie, like us" (*Shields Daily News*, March 20, 1952).[20]

That week, Stan met his sister Beatrice Olga's son for the first time. Huntley Jefferson Woods recalled:

> I approached the meeting with "Uncle Stan" with mixed feelings. After all, I didn't know what the reaction of such a famous star would be — even to a relation — especially as he had never seen me and knew me by name only. As it turned out, he was pleased to see me, and showed interest in my musical career. I also met his wife, who was equally charming. All in all, a marvellous night, which I shall always cherish [Marriot, 1993, pp. 173–74].

This is the paddle-driven "ha'penny" dodger passenger-only ferry which ran between North and South Shields when Stan lived in the town and about which he made many affectionate references in later years. It was the way in which Stan as a boy would have crossed the river to visit his father's theater in Hebburn. He could have used a passenger-only or a vehicular ferry when he crossed from North to South Shields en route to the Sunderland Empire in 1952. (North Tyneside Local Studies Library.)

Of his overall impression of "Uncle Stan," he added: "A great man, with the common touch."

During the following week, for their appearance at the Sunderland Empire, Stan and Oliver were driven down to the quayside at North Shields where they had to cross the river by ferry to South Shields before continuing on to Sunderland. Each night they made the reverse journey back to the Grand Hotel. (Not until 1967 was it possible to drive under the river via the Tyne Tunnel.) One night backstage in Sunderland, Stan met someone from his early theatrical days with the Levy Cardwell Juvenile Pantomime Company. Seventy-year-old Benny Barron, who had been in *Sleeping Beauty* with Stan, spent time reminiscing while waiting for the start of rehearsals. Afterwards, Stan told a reporter from the *Sunderland Echo*:

> And they were grand times. The money wasn't much but we were happy all the same. I remember playing in Sunderland years ago — was it the Villiers Institute? Times have changed a lot since then though, but there's one thing that remains the same — Northern audiences. They're wonderful [quoted by Marriot, 1993, p. 174].

After Tyneside and Wearside, Stan and Oliver moved on to Hanley, Leeds and then Nottingham — which gave Stan an opportunity to spend more time with his sister Olga who with her husband was running a pub in the area. Engagements then followed in Shrewsbury, Edinburgh, Southampton, Liverpool and Dublin. At that point they took a break — in Stan's case, an enforced break, to stabilize his diabetic condition. From Dublin they went on to Sheffield, Brighton, Manchester, Rhyl, Bradford, Coventry, Southport, Sutton, Bristol and Portsmouth. It was a tiring schedule and it was beginning to affect them. The packed theater in Portsmouth gave them a very good reception but one observer noted that although "their age did not appear to have diminished their skills ... they were really on their last legs — completely worn out" (Marriot, 1993, p. 205).

It was hardly surprising. They had been doing 13 shows a week for 27 weeks. They had criss-crossed England, Scotland and Wales, made many additional public appearances and stayed behind after shows to meet their fans. But the show had to go on: to Dudley, Swansea, and Cardiff. Finally, before returning home, they enjoyed an evening in the audience at the Prince of Wales theater in London to see the then up-and-coming comic Norman Wisdom.[21]

They returned to the U.S. on October 19. In less than a year, they were back in England again.

1953: Nearing the End

There is no record of Stan having visited North Shields in 1953. Nevertheless, the 1953 tour cannot be ignored because it proved to be the finale of Laurel and Hardy's 25-year career together. They began their tour in Ireland, where they had a huge, emotional welcome. Their first appearance in England was in Northampton, where things went well and they received a lot of publicity. However, the tour was not to continue on such a high note. The press in Liverpool seemed to have decided that their arrival in the city was not worth a mention and, more generally, the theater critics seemed to have made up their mind that the public's taste for comedy was changing. But it was not just changing tastes in comedy that were taking their toll. So too were Stan and Oliver's ages and health. The comedian and impressionist Peter Goodwright made these telling observations on their performance at Manchester:

> Their welcome on this occasion was fairly enthusiastic, but contained none of the euphoria of the previous appearance. This time the house was not full and Stan and Ollie had to work very hard for their laughs. It was on this occasion, as Laurel and Hardy took their applause that I realised, for the very first time, that I had been watching two men who were no longer young. As they stood on the stage, Stan looked gaunt with thinning hair, and Ollie was obviously having difficulty in walking. It came as a shock to me, I recall, and I was filled with a sadness that not even the laughter they had created could erase. I remember thinking "I shall not see them again," and of course, I never did. No one has emerged to take their place, but then — who could? [Goodwright interviewed by A.J. Marriot, 1993, p. 222].

During the following week, Stan was too ill to appear at the Finsbury Park Empire. Then, just as Stan was recovering from his serious upper respiratory infection which had left him temporarily deaf, Oliver had a very bad heart scare. Unwisely, he followed the old theatrical credo that "the show must go on" and did not go into hospital. Despite their bouts of illness, they both put on a good show in Newcastle. When a reporter for the *Shields Evening News* phoned Stan (back at the Royal Station Hotel again), he replied in a Geordie accent, "How're y' keepin?" When asked if he would be visiting North Shields during his week in the area, Stan replied, "I'll probably be down one of these days ... if so, I'll give you a call." He never did make that call and there is no documented evidence that Stan ventured down to the coast to North Shields on this occasion. It remains possible, of course, that he chose to do so quietly and without publicity.

Laurel and Hardy went on from Newcastle to Birmingham where the audience seemed to love their comedy sketch although the critics were cool. From Hull they went to Nottingham to appear in the Laurel and Hardy Christmas Show. They did three shows a day, instead of the usual two, and additional long tiring sessions with the children in the audience. By the time they reached Portsmouth, they were glad to return to just two shows a day but by then Oliver was really too ill for even that. And so their relentless schedule went on, show after show after show. Receiving surprisingly mixed receptions and reviews must have added to their personal woes. When they reached Plymouth in May, Oliver fell ill again and the whole of the week's performances had to be cancelled. As well as suffering from a nasty virus, he was diagnosed as having had a mild heart attack. When the full extent of his health problems became clear, the last week's engagements were also cancelled. The final curtain had come down on Laurel and Hardy's wonderful career.[22]

On May 30, 1954, Laurel and Hardy left Britain never to return. When they first arrived in Britain to a tumultuous welcome in 1932 it was on the luxury liner *Aquitania,* the most revered ship in the Cunard fleet, with exquisite interiors which earned it the nickname "The Ship Beautiful." It carried well over 3,000 passengers, 600 of them in first class. When they sailed unnoticed from Hull in 1954, it was on the Danish merchant ship *Manchuria.* It carried a maximum of 12 passengers, none in what would be regarded as first class accommodations. But it was not quite the ignominious retreat it might first appear. Stan described the journey back to the U.S. like this.

> We sailed from Hull Eng. June 3rd. on a Danish Cargo ship, the voyage took 23 days, stopped in at St. Thomas (Virgin Islands), Curacao, Christobal & through the Panama Canal. It was very interesting, especially the Canal. The accommodations were very nice — good food & calm sea all the

way, I really prefer traveling this way as you do'nt have to dress up for meals etc. as you do on the big passenger ships. There was only 10 passengers on this trip (12 is the limit they carry) so its practically like being on a private yacht.

Stan and Oliver's health improved on their return to the United States — but only for a short time. In 1955, while in advanced negotiations to make four TV films with Hal Roach, Stan had a stroke. Although he made a good recovery, he was dogged with bad health for the rest of his life. Despite his continuing heart problems, Oliver was able to visit Stan but he then succumbed to a severe stroke in 1956, from which he never did recover. He died on August 7, 1957. Stan lived for another seven years and died on February 23, 1965, at age 74.

1989: A Perilous Return to North Shields

North Shields gave Stan a wonderful ten years as a boy, and memories to draw on for the rest of his life. In return, Stan provided the canny folks of Shields with a famous yet unassuming hero of whom they could be justly proud. Yet the County Borough of Tynemouth, by the time it had disappeared with local government reorganization in 1974, had not only missed the opportunity to give him the Freedom of the Borough during his visits in 1932, 1947 and 1952; it had also done nothing tangible to mark the association between Stan Laurel and his boyhood town. The site of the demolished Theatre Royal remained a piece of waste ground throughout the whole of my boyhood. It could have been used in some way to symbolize the association between Stan Laurel and North Shields but instead it remained an eyesore, just around the corner from the workplace of the same mayor of Tynemouth who had been happy to share the stage with Stan at the charity concert they had both attended in 1952.

Still, better late than never, a tangible reminder of Stan's association with North Shields appeared in 1992. It stands, appropriately, in the new (mark III) Dockwray Square thanks to Persimmon Homes who commissioned it from the multi-talented South Shields artist Bob Olley. Had Stan still been with us, he would no doubt have transformed the story of how it left Bob's studio, and finished up on its plinth in Dockwray Square, into another Oscar-winning cinema classic.[23]

Bob began work on the statue in 1989. When the work was half-completed, the UK economy went into a deep recession and the building industry was badly hit. Persimmon Homes' cash flow was so stretched that it asked Bob to stop work on the project until their situation improved. Bob waved goodbye to the half-finished Stan, leaving him alone in his workshop, while he took himself off to Australia for three months (celebrating his 50th birthday on the way). In due course, Bob was given the green light to go ahead with the project but it was not until March 1992 that his sculpture was completed and the statue ready to be placed in Dockwray Square. In the real Stan's boyhood days, he would have made the river crossing from South Shields to North Shields on the "half-penny dodger" ferry. However, even the ferry's 1992 successor was not a suitable form of transport for a 12 feet Stan-lookalike weighing half a ton.

Just as the *Music Box* piano was heavy and difficult to move, so too was Stan's statue. It did not have had to be carried bodily up the steep stairs that still line the North Shields bankside, but it did have to be transported across the River Tyne. Just as Laurel and Hardy had to endure cameramen recording their every action, Bob knew that his efforts would also be recorded for posterity. However, he was determined to write his own script and made the arrangements for the crossing without consulting Persimmon's PR agency. His plan was to have the statue manhandled from his workshop onto the South Shields quayside where a mobile crane would lift it onto a barge. A small tug would then pull it across the river where another crane would lift it off and then onto a flat back lorry to take it up the steep hill to Dockwray Square, on the final leg of its journey.

"Mr. Fixit" was Bob's friend Big Alex — surely an ideal role for Oliver Hardy, who would have elected himself to the position by pointing to his chest with that characteristic flourish of his index finger. Big Alex took it upon himself to organize the whole operation: the cranes, barge, tug, lorry and even the presence of the harbor master to ensure a smooth crossing of the river. The morning for the crossing was chosen specifically because the tide would be at its highest.

A posse of reporters gathered on the quay at South Shields to report on the event as it unfolded. With them was a young, extremely nervous girl from the Persimmon's Public Relations agency. It was her first assignment. She needed constant reassurance that all would go according to plan. Bob was happy to give it. After all, his friend Big Alex was in charge. It was only after he had reassured her that Bob noticed that the anticipated TV cameras had not arrived. When he set the date, he could not have known that the famous soccer star Kevin Keegan was signing on as manager of Newcastle United (for the first time) and that a man who had shot and killed a local government officer in a planning dispute was making his first appearance in court.

But it was not only the TV crews who were missing. There was still no sign of the barge. As the reporters became restless, and the PR girl continued pacing up and down, Big Alex walked towards Bob, puffing on a cigarette and, as nonchalantly as the occasion allowed, informed him that the expected barge would not be arriving. It had been sent up river on another job! Fortunately, on learning of the problem, Big Alex had arranged an alternative: a tug that could replace it—provided it could get close enough to the quay before the tide began to drop. On hearing this latest update, the PR girl went ashen and the impatient reporters and photographers became restless. While placating them with coffee, Bob was relieved to hear a cheer. A tug had been spotted, chugging round the bend of the river.

It was much larger than the anticipated barge, and Bob was not confident it could do the job. Big Alex, ever the optimist, merely shrugged his shoulders and said, "Don't worry." As the tug maneuvered alongside the quay, Bob realized that they were missing something else. He asked Alex how long it would be before the crane arrived. Big Alex gave him a puzzled look, and asked, "What crane?" At that, the PR girl let out a sound comparable to the famous Stan Laurel whimper and visibly wobbled. Rising to the occasion, Bob seized the initiative and in an authoritative manner worthy of Oliver Hardy whispered a firm command to Big Alex, "Get me a crane!"

Using a ship-to-shore phone on the tug, Big Alex contacted the pilot boat waiting in the middle of the river and requested that it go to the quay at *North* Shields and tell the crane driver to get over to *South* Shields via the Tyne Tunnel. It was just as well that high tide was not due during the morning or evening rush hours that day or the whole event would have had to have been postponed. Fortunately, the driver had a clear run, and twenty minutes later he was arranging the lifting straps around the Stan Laurel statue.

At last everything began to fall into place. The reporters were scribbling away and the photographers arranging people for their shots. The PR girl began to regain her composure and color. For a time, it all went like clockwork. But as Bob boarded the tug, the skipper beckoned him to the wheelhouse to tell him some bad news. The tide was now on the turn and had retreated so far that the tug was aground. His only hope of getting the tug off would be to wait for a swell from a passing ship. Even then, he would have to give the tug's powerful engines "full ahead" to guarantee it would get off the river bed. While he was reasonably confident that he could manage that, there was still a very big snag. As the tug lurched forward on the swell, it was quite likely that the statue would topple over, go over the side and finish up in the river! As Bob worried about the fate

"Stan Laurel" crossing the Tyne from South Shields to North Shields in 1992. (Courtesy of Bob Olley, the South Shields artist and sculptor who created both this statue and the sculpture of Stan Laurel in Bishop Auckland.)

"Stan Laurel" being returned to his home in Dockwray Square, North Shields in 1992. (Courtesy of Bob Olley, the South Shields artist and sculptor who created both this statue and the sculpture of Stan Laurel in Bishop Auckland.)

of his over two-years-in-the-making creation, he wondered how the real Stan and Ollie would have responded to the situation. He felt sure that for the first time in his life it would have been Stan who turned to Ollie (in the guise of Big Alex) to utter the immortal phrase, "Well, here's another nice mess you've gotten me into!"

With the statue secured to the deck as well as they could manage in the short time available, they waited for a swell. When it came, the tug rose from the river bed, the twin diesel engines roared into action and the boat shuddered from stem to stern. As Olley recalls, "With one eye anxiously on the statue I gave the PR girl a reassuring wave as the vessel freed itself and shot off into the middle of the river." The statue wobbled ominously but held firm and Stan Laurel, wearing a bemused but still smiling expression, crossed the River Tyne for the very last time.

The crane driver, no doubt enjoying the excuse to play at being a Formula One racing driver for the day, revved his engine and sped back toward the Tyne Tunnel and North Shields.

Things went altogether more smoothly in North Shields. The mobile crane was waiting for the tug as it arrived on the northern bank of the river. The statue was lifted from the tug, lowered and secured onto a lorry and then driven the half-mile uphill. While making a turn at the steepest part of the hill, Stan's statue leaned at an angle of almost 45 degrees, but the straps holding him took the strain and he arrived in Dockwray Square still intact. He was then lifted into the air and carefully lowered onto the sandstone plinth waiting to receive him. Anxious hands coaxed him into his final position. Stan was home at last, looking as if he was thinking, "How on earth did I get back here?" Olley's expression was entirely different: one of great and obvious relief.

When Bob next encountered the PR girl at the unveiling ceremony, she asked him if he had ever been worried about the transportation of Stan's statue. He lied!

The Stan Laurel statue was unveiled on March 29, 1992, by the local Member of Parliament. It is one of three in the north of England. A second, also sculpted by Olley, was commissioned by Wear Valley District Council. It had a longer journey to make to its Bishop Auckland destination and was also threatened by calamities. After visiting the Sichuan foundry in China owned by his friend Lu Huagang, Olley was so impressed with the quality of the workmanship that he went there to complete his design. He then returned to the UK while the statue was cast. But in May 2008, the country was hit by the devastating Sichuan earthquake, which measured 7.9 on the Richter scale, with its epicenter just 25 miles away from the factory. Tens of thousands of people died, millions were left homeless, and the factory suffered damage. Bob's statue of Stan somehow survived unscathed. Even then, the risk to the life-size statue was not over because it was caught up in a typhoon as it was transported the 11,500 miles to England. It was erected on the site of Arthur Jefferson's Eden Theatre and unveiled by Stan's cousin Nancy Wardell on August 30, 2008. The third statue, a life-size bronze of Laurel and Hardy by Graham Ibbeson, was erected outside Ulverston's Coronation Hall Theatre on April 19, 2009, by the veteran comedian Ken Dodd. In addition to these three statues, life-size silhouettes of Laurel and Hardy stare out at the sea on the promenade at Redcar, also in the northeast of England.

So, while Stan Laurel may have died in 1965, and his body may have been laid to rest at Forest Lawn, Hollywood Hills Cemetery, in Los Angeles, 5,000 miles away from his boyhood homes, his memory lives on: in the form of statues in the towns in which he lived as a boy; in the memories of all those who loved and admired him around the world; and, most of all, in the enduring films he made with his incomparable partner Oliver Hardy. The timeless, universal qualities of their films have made people laugh for the last 85 years and they will continue to do so for as long as we are privileged to have access to them.

Epilogue

In today's entertainment world, anyone who has appeared on UK TV, doing nothing more significant than picking his or her nose on a so-called reality show such as *Big Brother*, seems destined to become "a celebrity." Anyone who appears on TV regularly is termed a "star." People of only modest achievements in the UK are given honorary degrees, knighthoods and even peerages. So, one inevitably wonders how Stan Laurel would have fared had the same standards been in operation when he was at the peak of his international fame.

There seems no doubt that Stan and Oliver would have been described as mega-stars or some other such term devised by those responsible for marketing hype. They would have been showered with offers of honorary degrees. And someone of the stature and popularity of Stan, who never gave up his British citizenship, would surely have been awarded a peerage. I like to think that he would have chosen for his title: Lord Laurel of Shields.[1]

Appendix

Theaters Played During the UK Tours[1]

Moss Empire theaters are **bold**.
P = played. B = booked but not played.

Theater	*1947*	*1952*	*1953–4*
Belfast Grand Opera House		P	
Birmingham Aston Hippodrome			P
Birmingham Hippodrome	P	P	P
Blackpool Palace	P		
Bolton Lido	P		
Boscombe Hippodrome	P		
Bradford Alhambra		P	P
Brighton Hippodrome		P	P
Bristol Hippodrome	P	P	
Cardiff New Theatre		P	
Carlisle Her Majesty's			P
Coventry Hippodrome	P	P	
Dublin Olympia		P	P
Dudley Hippodrome	P	P	
Edinburgh Empire	P	P	P
Glasgow Empire	P	P	P
Grimsby Palace			P
Hanley Royal		P	
Hull New Theatre	P		
Hull Palace			P
Leeds Empire		P	P
Liverpool Empire	P	P	P
London Brixton Empress			P
London Chiswick Empire	P		P
London Coliseum	P		
London, Finsbury Park Empire	P		P
London Lewisham Hippodrome	P		

Appendix

Theater	1947	1952	1953–4
London Palladium	P		
London Victoria Palace	P		
London Wimbledon	P		
Manchester Hippodrome			P
Manchester Palace	**P**	**P**	
Margate Winter Gardens	P		
Morecambe Victoria Palace	P		
Newcastle Empire	**P**	**P**	**P**
Northampton New Theatre			P
Norwich Hippodrome			P
Nottingham Empire		**P**	**P**
Peterborough Embassy		P	
Plymouth Palace			P
Portsmouth Royal		P	P
Rhyl Queen's		P	
Sheffield Empire		**P**	**P**
Shrewsbury Granada		P	
Skegness Butlin's Gaiety	P		
Southampton Gaumont		P	
Southend Odeon		P	
Southport Garrick		P	
Southsea King's	P		
Sunderland Empire		**P**	**P**
Sutton Granada		P	
Swansea Empire		**P**	**B**
Swindon Empire	P		
Wolverhampton Hippodrome			P
York Empire			P
Total	*24*	*28*	*27*

Chapter Notes

Chapter 1

1. It was later re-roofed and modernized. At that stage, it seated 1,400 people, had a pit, boxes and gallery and was lit by electricity. It burned down in 1910.

2. In the 1881 census, George Metcalfe was described as a shoemaker *and* general dealer (i.e., the owner of a small shop or store selling a variety of items, mainly of the kind bought on a daily basis).

3. Initially he had a partner, Thomas Thore, but from 1901 he ran it alone. In other records, his partner's surname is recorded as Thorne.

4. Baptism at home is allowed for in situations of "grave cause and necessity." In such extreme cases, "no minister being informed of the weakness or danger of death of any infant within his cure and therefore desired to go to baptize the same shall either refuse or delay to do so (canon B22 [6] of the Church of England). Stanley was later "received into the church" in a ceremony at St. Peter's Church, Bishop Auckland, on October 21, 1891.

5. Originally, a Dutch *stoep* was a covered porch with seats, as introduced by the Dutch into New York. Subsequently, it became a term for an outdoors flight of stairs with a platform, leading to an entrance door some distance above the street. Still later, the term was used to describe any porch, platform, entrance stairway, or small veranda at the door of the house.

6. Andrew Gough is the unnamed email correspondent in Stella Colwell's account of Stan Laurel's family background (Colwell, 2003, p. 267).

7. There is reason to suppose that Alexander had tired of Harriet when he moved on to his second mistress, Fanny Morgan, but he continued to see Fanny while enjoying the companionship of Bessie King. When he died at his so-called London residence in 1892, it was in the same Gloucester Place house where Fanny resided until her then-recent death. Alexander was in the company of Bessie King, at a hotel in Preston, in 1871 and staying at her home (albeit in the company of her father) in 1891. Whether or not their relationship was platonic, it was sufficiently close for him to leave her a substantial legacy. Expressed in terms of relative share of GDP, the £150 he left her would be worth the equivalent of £154,000 today. In addition, he left her the annual income from a £3,000 investment, the equivalent of over £3 million in 2008. See footnote 8 for an explanation of why this particular inflation indicator has been adopted.

8. All price comparisons in this book are based on the excellent website: http://www.measuringworth.com/thanks.html. Of the several inflation measures available, this seems the most appropriate although the particular example cited uses two individuals living in different periods: "Sometimes you want to know how very rich people compare.

Recently it was reported that Warren Buffet is the richest person in the world and is worth $52 billion today. When John D. Rockefeller died in 1937 he was worth $1.4 billion. Who is richer in their time? … The question … can be best measured by how big their wealth is compared to the economy they live(d) in. This is measured by share of GDP and for Rockefeller, that number is $210 billion, or four times greater that Mr. Buffet."

9. Wilson was Harriet's maiden name.

10. The birth of an Arthur Jefferson was registered in Darlington in the fourth quarter of 1862 but it is readily apparent from the 1871 census that he belongs to an entirely different family. The same holds true for the three Arthur Goughs registered in quarters three and four of 1862.

11. For more information on the careers of T.C. King, his daughter Katty and her husband Arthur Lloyd, see the following web pages: http://www.arthurlloyd.co.uk/Ancestry/TCKing.htm; http://www.arthurlloyd.co.uk/Ancestry/Katty.htm; http://www.arthurlloyd.co.uk/ArthurLloydBiography.htm

Chapter 2

1. It is not possible to make a definitive statement about when Arthur Jefferson arrived in North Shields or when he made his home in the town. He announced in a public meeting in 1901 that he had been in the town for seven years, suggesting a date of 1894, which is consistent with his being in control of the Theatre Royal in 1895.

2. Jefferson Street in Blyth was named in honor of A.J. When it was demolished in 1989, the name plate was saved thanks to the combined intervention of Stan Laurel's nephew, Huntley Jefferson Woods (a resident of Blyth), and a sympathetic local councilor (*Evening Chronicle,* April 24, 1989).

3. For a history of North Shields, see my forthcoming book *Shiels to Shields: The Life Story of an English Seaport.*

4. Kean's appearance was comparable to someone like Sir Laurence Olivier appearing in North Shields at the peak of his career in the 20th century: something which not only did not happen but which was also inconceivable.

5. It is indicative of the period that a subsequent letter to the *Shields Daily News* asked that the planned return visit be on a week night "as many would not like to attend on a Sunday, especially in a theatre" (*Shields Daily News,* November 11, 1885).

6. The theater was on the Pipemaker's Stairs, near what today is Borough Bank. It would appear that the Delavals had a long-standing interest in the theater. Sir Francis Delaval, MP, born in 1727, not only attended the theater and put on amateur productions at Delaval Hall but even produced Shakespeare's *Othello* at Drury Lane Theatre with himself in the title role and family members in the cast. It seems that the House of Commons adjourned early so that MPs could attend. Sir Francis lived such an eccentric and racy life that it inspired the writer and TV producer Roger Burgess to feature him in two BBC-TV drama documentaries. In 2007, after an interval of over 30 years, he and Bob Jeffrey turned the material into a musical titled *Those Delavals!* It was staged at Tynemouth Priory Theatre in April 2007. Seaton Delaval Hall has now become the property of the National Trust.

7. The area developed was between the Bank Top, Tynemouth Road, Norfolk Street and Bedford Street. The theater was built at the junction of Howard Street with Union Street. The Pipemaker's Stairs theater closed in 1798 and two years later it was being used as a meeting house for a dissenting religious group (King, 1947, p. 34).

8. George Osmond Tearle was so well known that his death was reported in the *New York Times* of September 8, 1901. He was buried in St. Paul's Church in nearby Whitley Bay.

9. G.J. Mellor in *Picture Pioneers—The Story of the Northern Cinemas 1896–1971* makes no mention of A.J. Jefferson but does refer to Poole's Myriorama in association with the Howard Hall in North Shields.

10. They showed films in the wooden building between 1906 and 1910 when it was destroyed by a disastrous fire. Within six months they had rebuilt it as a modern, well-equipped theater. George Black Jr., son of the original proprietor of the Borough, went on to found Black's Picture Enterprises. His brother Alfred, who had also served his cinematic apprenticeship under his father at the North Shields Borough, went on to run what eventually became a large national operation. George Jr., at a later stage when director of the General Theatre Corporation, merged it with Moss Empires in 1932, giving him control of most of Britain's best music halls, earning him the nickname "Emperor of Variety" at a time when variety was very big business. On nine occasions Black organized the Royal Variety Command Performance at the London Palladium. It was because of the connection between the Jefferson and Black families that Stan opened his first UK variety tour at the Moss Empire Theatre in Newcastle upon Tyne in 1947. Just as A.J. had been obliged to confront the competition between live theater and cinema, Black was obliged to confront the perceived competition between live theater and radio. He chose to live with it rather than fight against it. Fortnightly radio transmissions from his London Palladium began in October 1928. They were popular with listeners but met with opposition from the Variety Artistes' Federation, even though individual performers earned an additional fee if their performance was broadcast (Asa Briggs, *History of Broadcasting in the UK*, 1995, pp. 76–79).

11. See the Gould Gazetteer of Provincial Theatres and Music Halls on the Mercia Cinema Society website: http://merciacinema.org.

12. The plans for the conversion were drawn up by William Stockdale of Howard Street, North Shields, for Messrs. Atkinson and Browell. A copy of the Specification and Bill of Quantities has survived and can be found in the Local Studies Library in North Shields. The intention was to "entirely demolish all the premises known as the Theatre Royal together with a portion of the buildings at the rear of the shops and house and to erect a cinema with a variety stage." The site remained derelict for many years, though occasionally used for small temporary fairground attractions. It was eventually used for a block of flats in the closing decades of the twentieth century.

Chapter 3

1. He could, of course, have been a resident in 1894 as he implied in his 1901 speech but been too preoccupied with other matters to have completed the registration form. I am grateful to my old friend and colleague Eric Rowe for drawing my attention to the terms of the 1884 Representation of the People Act. Readers should note that, in this early period, UK registers are of limited value in identifying local residents. Even by 1911, only about 60 percent of adult males were eligible to vote. The right to vote was not conceded to all women over the age of 21 until 1928.

2. Some writers describe him as the vicar of Tynemouth. That is not the case. There have been two vicars of Christ Church called Thomas Dockwray. The first served between 1668 and 1673. He was succeeded by his son Stephen. On his death in 1681, the position

passed to his brother Thomas. The latter died in 1724. During the period when Thomas Dockwray began developing his land in North Shields in 1763, the Christ Church vicar (from 1749 to 1789) was Emmanuel Potter.

3. It has been suggested that stones purloined from the ruins of Tynemouth Priory were used in the construction of Dockwray Square. See, for example, *Saturday Review*, Vol. 4, 1834, p. 3.

4. Stan himself suffered a similar ordeal in 1930. His only son, Stan Laurel Jr., lived for only a few days.

5. Arthur Jefferson was listed on the electoral roll for Dockwray Square in October 1902 but Ayton House, Ayre's Terrace in October 1903.

Chapter 4

1. This was a period when most children in England received only a very limited education and large sections of the adult population were functionally illiterate. At the time of Stan's birth, education was provided for the majority by a mixture of voluntary and local government schools. Although attendance was made compulsory in 1880, it ended at the age of 13. Only families with the means to pay could provide their children with the kind of education which Stan enjoyed (or, to be more accurate, did not enjoy).

2. At 60 Jesmond Road, Newcastle, between 1894 and 1899. James Gordon was 39 in 1901, still unmarried, and living with his retired, Scottish-born schoolmaster father John Gordon (age 62) and his mother Margaret (age 72). His address in 1909 was 1 Tynemouth Place, Tynemouth. He died on January 20, 1915, at age 54.

3. Readers are reminded that in all instances where Stan's written words are quoted, they have been transcribed with his own, idiosyncratic punctuation.

4. King's School was first established in 1860 by the Rev. Thomas White. After several early changes it was named Tynemouth School; in 1961 it became known as King's School. Staff and student numbers are not available for the time Stan appears to have attended but in 1899 it is known to have had four teachers in addition to the headmaster and there were 65 pupils on the school roll (John H. Taylor, *The King's School Tynemouth — A History*).

5. The Laurel Building named in honor of its short-lived former pupil, which lay unused for some years, was so damaged by a 2007 fire that it was announced that it was to be sold off for commercial development (*Northern Echo*, December 27, 2008).

6. Streets around the country were named after the event. My own paternal grandfather was living at 6 Mafeking Terrace in the nearby village of New York when he died in 1908.

7. The *Wellesley* was a training ship moored in the river off North Shields. Like other such ships elsewhere in the UK, it provided training for "needy" boys so that they would prove suitable recruits for the Royal and Merchant Navies.

8. Limelight was a type of stage lighting in use during this period, particularly in theaters and music halls. Brilliant light was created by playing an oxy-hydrogen flame on a cylinder of calcium oxide (quick lime). The still-used expression that someone is "in the limelight" is a legacy of that chemical process.

9. His father suggested that Stan was then "about nine years of age" but does not correspond with the fact that the theater was created in Ayton House and the Jeffersons were still living in Dockwray Square in 1901 when Stan was approaching his 11th birthday.

Chapter 5

1. Precisely when she died is uncertain. Owen-Pawson and Mouland offer the date of her death as September 1, 1908 (Owen-Pawson and Mouland, 1984, p. 101). Louvish states the date of death was December 1, 1908 (Louvish, 2001 p. 49). My own searches on http://www.scotlandspeople.gov.uk have so far failed to find corroboration for either date but the latter seems the more likely because the *Tyneside Weekly News* reported her death as "last weekend" on December 11, 1908. Arthur Jefferson married a 40-year-old widow, Venetia Matilda Robinson, on November 14, 1912. He died in 1949 at an uncertain age which reflects the uncertainty over the date of his birth.

2. Pickard was a genuine eccentric with a zany sense of humor. Apparently he would sit on the top of a ladder at the side of the stage throwing nails at disorderly members of the audience. If he thought an act not good enough, he would drag them from the stage by the use of a long pole with a hook on the end — to the delight of the audience. Stan not only escaped that indignity but, at a time when Glasgow audiences had a reputation for being the most difficult in the country, earned himself a good reception.

3. In 1987, STV produced a half-hour play called *Stan's First Night*, about his appearance on stage that evening. The original Britannia Music Hall, in the Trongate area of Glasgow, opened in 1857 and closed in 1903. Three years later, it re-opened as the Britannia Theatre of Varieties and Panopticon. It closed in 1938 but was not demolished and at the time of writing is undergoing a major restoration.

4. The first Royal Command Performance took place on July 1, 1912, at the Palace Theatre in London's West End. King George V and Queen Mary attended. It was a lavish occasion and it is claimed, however improbably, that the theater was decorated with as many as three million roses. The performers were a mixed lot. They included the music hall artiste Vesta Tilley and, in marked contrast, the Russian ballerina Anna Pavlova. The only recorded embarrassment occurred when Tilley appeared on stage. Apparently Queen Mary buried her face in her program, not because Tilley was immodestly dressed but because she was wearing trousers. That did not become commonplace and acceptable until Britain was confronted with the unprecedented circumstances of the First World War when large numbers of women were obliged to take on what had previously been men's work.

5. Both received unlikely recognition from the Beatles. Wee Georgie Wood is mentioned in a track ("Dig It") on the album *Let It Be* and Stan Laurel features on the cover montage of their *Sergeant Pepper* album. Unlike Stan, Wee Georgie Wood also received recognition from the British Establishment when he was awarded an O.B.E (Officer in the Most Excellent Order of the British Empire) in 1946.

6. Stan later rewrote the sketch and turned it into what some regard as the first "proper" Laurel and Hardy film *Duck Soup*. It was later remade as the sound film *Another Fine Mess*. Stan's father is credited with the story.

7. She appears to have died on December 1 and the opening night was on the 7th.

8. Stan's week of glory was in the Ealing and Willesden Hippodromes in the week beginning Monday, April 18, 1910. Both future stars had heavenly competition that week from Halley's Comet which reached its perihelion on Wednesday the 20th, its closest approach to the Sun since 1835.

9. The *Lusitania* was torpedoed off Ireland in 1915. Over a thousand passengers and crew died.

10. It has been suggested that the Chaplin role that appealed to Sennett, and formed

the basis of Chaplin's future success, was *Jimmy the Intrepid*, a character devised by Stan when they were living and working together as part of the Fred Karno company.

11. Including Abjhazia, Angola, Burkina Faso, France, Fujeira, Gambia, Guyana, Karakalpakia, Romania, the UK and USA. The following list gives the names of Laurel and Hardy as they are known in different countries: in Albania, Olio me Stelion; Brazil, O Gordo e o Magro; Denmark, Gog and Cokke; Egypt, El Tikhin Ouel Roufain; Estonia, Laurel ja Hardy or Paks ja Peenike; Finland, Ohukainen Ja Paksuinen; France, Laurel et Hardy; Galicia area, Laurel e Hardy or O Gordo e o Fraco; Germany, Laurel und Hardy or Stan und Ollie or Dick und Doof; Greece, Xonapoe and Azsnoe or Chondros Kai Lighnos; Hungary, Stan es Pan; Iceland, Steini og Olli; Israel, Hashamen ve Haraze; Italy, Stanlio e Ollio or Crik and Crok; Korea, Hol-jjug-i wa Dkung-ddung-i; Kurdistan, Laurel u Hardy; Malta, L-Ohxon u l-Irqiq; Norway, Helan og Halvan; Poland, Flip i Flap; Portugal, O Bucha or O Estica; Romania, Stan and Bran; Serbia, Stanlio i Olio; Spain, El Gordo y el Flaco; Sweden / Norway, Helan and Halvan; The Netherlands, De Dikke en de Dunne; Turkey, Sisman ve Zaif and UK, USA and other English speaking countries, Laurel and Hardy. Courtesy of Stephen Neale's *Crazy World of Laurel and Hardy* website: http://www.stanlaurelandoliverhardy.com/index.htm

12. One of only two films *made* in color. According to Stan, their only color film was the lost 1930 *Rogue Song* in which they played supporting roles. Many of their films are now available in a computer-generated color format. This process of colorization is understandably unpopular with purists and with film historians but, arguably, if it makes the films more acceptable to young people who take color for granted, then the process will have served its immediate purpose.

13. Figures compiled by Hal Roach indicate that during the production, the studio used over 1,700 gallons of paint and varnish weighing over 20,000 lbs.; 196,000 square feet of lumber weighing 588,000 lbs; 240,000 square feet of wall board; 192,000 square feet of plaster; 80,000 square feet of chicken wire; 80,000 square feet of burlap, 7,000 lbs. worth of nails. Almost three million watts of electricity were generated per hour to illuminate the sets. On completion of the picture, Roach gave the Toyland set to the City of Los Angeles to be erected in the Griffith Park children's playground. The film was reissued in later years under a variety of titles, including *March of the Wooden Soldiers*, *Laurel and Hardy in Toyland* and *March of the Toys*.

14. When *Great Guns* opened, the A film on the bill was French director Jean Renoir's *Swamp Water*. Orson Welles was later to describe Renoir as the greatest of all directors.

15. The cast included Ray Bolger, best known for his role as the Scarecrow in *The Wizard of Oz*. The emcee was John Garfield, who had recently been nominated for an Academy Award.

16. *The Tree in a Test Tube*, distributed by the U.S. government, was intended to make the public aware of the value of wood products, especially in wartime. Shot on 16mm Kodachrome film, it is especially noteworthy because it was shot in color when nearly all other Laurel and Hardy films were shot in monochrome — one of the reasons that most people are unaware that Stan had red hair. Unfortunately, the versions currently in circulation that I have seen have been so badly reproduced that there is virtually no color in evidence.

17. Mitchell suggests that the introduction of a stateless refugee into the plot may have come from the fact that John Berry, the film's assistant director, was an exile from the U.S., a victim of the McCarthy hearings designed to root out so-called communists.

18. Such apparently officious guidelines may have been because the film was subsidized by the French government (MacGillivray, 2008, p. 205).

19. MacGillivray quotes Stan Laurel's daughter Lois as saying that her father was very upset because he believed it had been agreed that it would not be released in the U.S. (MacGillivray, 2008, p. 213).

20. Stan had wanted his friend Jerry Lewis to accept the award for him but the Academy insisted on Kaye.

21. Stan himself played a gardener in two 1922 films, *The Weak-End Party* and *The Handy Man,* before he teamed with Oliver Hardy.

22. The 281st tent was formed in Ellenville, New York, in April 2009.

23. Tom McGrath, who was born in Rutherglen, Glasgow, where the then Stan Jefferson lived when he moved with his family from North Shields to Glasgow, died on April 29, 2009, just months before it opened.

Chapter 6

1. In that period, a 35mm motion picture reel of 1,000 feet ran for about 11 minutes at a sound speed (24 frames per second) and slightly longer at the silent movie speed (usually 16 to 18 frames per second). So-called "two-reeler" films ran about 20 to 24 minutes.

2. First class vessels means over 15 tons; second class less than 15 tons and third class with a keel less than 15 feet (Wright, 2002, p. 86).

3. It was still in operation during my childhood. Given an ill wind, the smell from the factory was awful.

4. A gold badge because of the size of the fish and the fact that it was caught in just 55 minutes fishing.

5. Stan was also partial to tripe and onions, another traditional northern English dish.

6. His screen character wore shoes without heels which helped make him look shorter and more vulnerable and also gave him his characteristic flip-flop gait.

7. Eton College was then and still is an élite school. As an example of its significance, 19 British prime ministers attended Eton, including David Cameron, the current UK Prime Minister, and many of his senior colleagues.

8. This embarrassing distinction between taller and shorter pupils was withdrawn in 1967. From then on all boys, whatever their height, went straight into tailcoats.

Chapter 7

1. Letter from Sylvester Blackett to the North Shields Local Studies Librarian Eric Hollerton, June 22, 1990. Sylvester, who was born and lived in North Shields at 82 Linskill Terrace, became a comedian using the stage name Vic Silver. He referred in his letter to other local comedians "like Stan Annise, Tommy Gibson, Adam Tomlinson, the Bernard Brothers, J. C. Scatter and Bobby Thompson, sadly all gone now."

2. The fourth Wooden Dolly survived for over 50 years, though by then it was badly disfigured by the continuing tradition of cutting slivers from her for good luck. Its replacement, Dolly #5, was carved in the same style as #4 but in 1958 was placed not on the Custom House Quay but as the centerpiece of Northumberland Square. It still stands there, overlooked by the Local Studies Library. However, when the Prince of Wales public house on Custom House Quay, North Shields, was saved from demolition in 1992, the brewers, Sam Smith of Tadcaster, returned a likeness of the third Dolly to the original site. So North Shields now has two Wooden Dollies. Alas, there are very few sailors now

using the port so (unless it is found to be in the way of yet another housing development) it should enjoy a longer life than its predecessors.

3. Hinney (also spelled hinny) is a term of endearment used in the Tyneside area. Readers interested in the Geordie dialect could consult George Todd's *Geordie Words and Phrases. An Aid to Communication on Tyneside and Thereabouts* (Frank Graham, 1977) or Chapter 10 of Simon Elmes' *Talking for Britain — A Journey Through the Nation's Dialects* (Penguin Books, 2005).

4. "Apenny" (i.e., half-penny) dip consisted of a cardboard tube of sherbet powder, eaten by dipping in the supplied stick of licorice. Variants are still available today. Black bullets were hard and round and made of boiled sugar, flavored with peppermint. Sold loose from big jars and served in paper bags, they were as popular in my day as they were in Stan's. Although they are still available, in these more hygiene-conscious days they are individually wrapped in the factory.

5. Stan obviously remembered that the people of North Shields usually refer to beaches as "the sands."

6. Stan often referred to his wife as Eda even though she is ordinarily referred to as Ida.

7. Stan lived in North Shields during an exciting time in the development of rail transport. The Newcastle and North Shields Railway Company had been running one of the world's first suburban passenger-carrying railways from as early as 1839. Other lines followed, including a line between North Shields and Tynemouth. When Stan first came to live in North Shields and travelled to school in Tynemouth, the carriages were pulled by steam locomotives. The lines were electrified, using a third rail carrying 600 volts DC and new rolling stock brought into operation in 1904, beating the electrification of the Mersey rail system by a few weeks. This huge transformation took place in the year before the Jeffersons left North Shields for Glasgow.

8. A proposal for a railway tunnel with a fast shuttle service of electric trains between Bedford Street in North Shields and Mile End Road in South Shields was put forward in 1902, when Stan was living in North Shields. The proposal received Parliamentary approval but was subsequently abandoned. The work on the much less ambitious project of a pedestrian and parallel cyclists' tunnel was eventually started in 1939 but brought to a halt by the Second World War; work recommenced in 1947 and completed in 1951. Stan's remarks about going through the tunnel in bare feet is a reminder that in his day many children went barefoot because their parents could not afford shoes for them. Stan's own parents raised substantial sums of money to ameliorate that situation. His lapses into the vernacular *gen* (go) and *yer* (your) are a reminder that he remained familiar with the Geordie accent to the end.

9. In this instance, Stan was a little out of touch. The Dodger had actually made its last journey between North and South Shields on August 28, 1954, after Stan's last visit, but before this letter was written. This small, passenger-only paddle steamer had been in service for 107 years. The initial fare was 1d. (i.e., 1 pre-decimal penny) but was soon lowered to ½ d. when it proved popular. It was nicknamed the *dodger* because of the way it dodged its way through other traffic on the river. A larger vehicular ferry between North and South Shields was introduced to cross later.

10. *Gaan* in the Geordie dialect is the equivalent of *going* in standard English.

11. Stan is referring to what has become known as the Munich Air Disaster in which BAE flight 609 crashed on its third attempt to take off from a slush-covered runway on February 6, 1958. It carried Manchester United's hugely talented Busby Babes soccer team. Twenty of the 44 passengers were killed.

12. A kipper is a smoked herring (created in huge numbers in North Shields in his day). The point of Stan's joke is that Geordies could never afford to eat pheasant, a game bird consumed only by the wealthy.

13. "Canny Aad Shields" is the Geordie dialect rendering of "Dear Old Shields." "Canny" is a multi-purpose term to Geordies but does not carry the pejorative connotation of being mean with money which it signifies when used by other people in England or Scotland. Stan's reference to Marden "town" is to the Marden housing estate. In his day, the whole of this area and much more besides was open green space.

Chapter 8

1. A major clearance of the bankside eventually started in 1933, shortly after Stan's visit in 1932.

2. At the time, there were several other cinemas in the Borough outside what Stan called the "old town" of North Shields.

3. I am grateful to my old friend George Thomson for digging out this information for me.

4. It was built in 1878 but proved to be a white elephant for much of its life. Conveniently (for its owners), it was badly damaged by fire and then demolished in 1996.

5. When King George V came to open the Tyne Bridge in 1928, he made a donation to pay for underprivileged children to have a day out at the coast. The *Evening Chronicle* adopted the idea of raising money to support local children in need and the fund was named the Sunshine Fund. Today, this registered northeast charity helps children in special schools, learning units and hospitals and also individual families in their homes by providing money for custom-built apparatus and specialized learning aids.

6. Newcastle's Moss Empire was demolished in 1963.

7. Durbin's emotional rendering of the song was set against a background of the UK's Union Jack and the United States' Stars and Stripes. To add more meaning to the words, she sang directly to the camera, as if actually appearing before the cinema audiences. A different but equally patriotic song, "I Give My Thanks to America," capped U.S. prints of *Nice Girl?* Clips of her renderings of the two songs are available at http://www.youtube.com/watch?v=qhUFVrdsd2A and http://www.youtube.com/watch?v=LIJAZeJ4W4s

8. The bombing of Wilkinson's shelter and many other incidents during the War are described in *North Shields: The Bombing of a Town* by Ron Curran (Curran, 2009).

9. Councilor Mavin was interested in the theater and would have relished his meeting with Stan and Oliver. He led the effort to revive the Tynemouth Amateur Operatic Society which had been suspended after the outbreak of war in 1939 and became its president in 1947. He remained in that post for the next 50 years.

10. In 1956, less than a decade later, and shortly after Stan's final visit in 1953, the Council declared Dockwray Square unfit for habitation and opted not for refurbishment but total demolition. The shoddily built council flats that replaced them lasted only a few decades. Then they too were demolished and replaced with the private housing that occupies the site today.

11. Central heating was a luxury which had not yet spread to even most of the middle class. In a typical working or middle class household, there would be a single coal fire in the living room. In cold weather, the fire would not be efficient enough to warm anything

other than the area immediately in front of it. Bedrooms, even those with grates, would remain unheated unless someone was ill and confined to bed.

12. By a curious coincidence, Stan was born in what became Argyll Street in Ulverston in 1890; made his first serious appearance on the stage in Argyll Street in Glasgow in 1906; and reached the pinnacle of his theatrical career in another Argyll Street when he and Oliver were invited to appear at the Royal Variety Performance at the London Palladium in 1947.

13. Oliver turned to straight acting: He toured in the stage play *What Price Glory?*; played a significant role in John Wayne's film *The Fighting Kentuckian*; and had a cameo in Bing Crosby's film *Riding High*.

14. Stan's ill health has already been described in Chapter 6. Oliver was found to have a heart condition during his stay abroad.

15. That still seems to be the case even if one allows for the fact that they also played the London Palladium and London Coliseum in 1947, and made slightly fewer appearances than in the 1952 and 1953 tours. See the Appendix for details of their engagements on their three tours.

16. I can confirm that the Grand Hotel did improve. My wife and I had our wedding reception there in 1966. It has since been extensively restored.

17. The concert was on behalf of cancer research and the widows and orphans fund of the National Union of Journalists. The bill opened with the Northumbrian Serenaders followed by Frankie Burns, Betty Hart, Tony Rowley, James Metcalf and Dick Irwin. The accompanist was Stan Phelps. (See *Shields Daily News*, March 15, 1952.) A police presence was needed to control the crowds, and numerous people who turned up hoping to see the show were turned away.

18. In November of the following year, at the age of 12, I appeared on that same Gaumont stage. In the first week I made seven brief solo appearances in the interval to publicize the following week's Gang Show. In the second I was part of a cast of 120 playing to seven full houses. For a young boy it was a thrilling experience, but knowing that I was treading the same boards on which Laurel and Hardy had stood the previous year made it even more exciting. The prodigious pianist Stan Phelps, the accompanist during the charity show, was also the accompanist for the Gang Show.

19. Matilda Harmon, William's daughter, recalled Stan's visit with affection on her 100th birthday (*Evening Chronicle*, November 1, 1991).

20. What is a Geordie? Two key elements are involved: being brought up in the area and having a sense of identity with the people who live there. In both that objective and subjective sense, I remain a Geordie even though I have not lived on Tyneside for many years. That was the meaning Stan was conveying to Harmon with his remark. There are at least four plausible explanations for how the term Geordie emerged. 1. During the Jacobite Rebellion of 1745, Newcastle declared itself "for George" (King George II) and the people of the area became known as Geordies. 2. Geordies are named after George Stephenson, the engineer and railway pioneer from the northeast because miners elsewhere adopted the Sir Humphrey Davy safety lamp while those in the area of the Tyne preferred Geordie's lamp, i.e., the lamp designed by George Stephenson. 3. After George Stephenson addressed a Parliamentary Commission in his distinctive local dialect, those with similar accents were dubbed Geordies. 4. The term derives from the music hall entertainer Geordie Ridley who wrote the Geordie equivalent of the national anthem, "The Blaydon Races."

21. The late Sir Norman went on to become a genuinely international star, helped

(like Laurel and Hardy) by the essentially visual nature of his comedy. Born in 1915, his last performance was in 2008 at the age of 92.

22. Their final public appearance together was in 1955, in a filmed interview for a BBC television program about a British variety organization, the Grand Order of Water Rats.

23. The account that follows is a revised version of Bob Olley's own description of the event on his website: http://www.robertolley.co.uk/StanLaurel/page2.html.

Appendix

1. Based on information in A.J Marriot's *Laurel & Hardy: The British Tours,* pp.286–301.

Epilogue

1. I have never understood why Stan was not afforded any official recognition by the British government. Perhaps if he had lived ten years longer, something would have come his way. A knighthood was first suggested for Charlie Chaplin in 1931 and again in 1956 but it was not agreed upon until he was 85 years old in 1975. Chaplin was also awarded an honorary degree by the University of Durham in 1962. Ironically, the University of Durham was then the nearest university to North Shields.

Bibliography

The literature on and available sources relating to the work and lives of Stan Laurel and Oliver Hardy continues to grow. Those interested in knowing more should consult the following books and Internet sources.

Books

Anobile, R. J. (1975). *The Best of Laurel & Hardy: Verbal and Visual Gems from "The Crazy World of Laurel & Hardy."* London: Michael Joseph.

Aping, N. (2008). *The Final Film of Laurel and Hardy: A Study of the Chaotic Making and Marketing of* Atoll K. Jefferson, NC: McFarland.

Barr, C. (1967). *Laurel & Hardy.* London, Studio Vista.

Bowers, J. (2007). *Stan Laurel and Other Stars of the Panopticon: The Story of the Britannia Music Hall.* Edinburgh: Birlinn.

Bradbury, Ray. (2002). *One More for the Road.* London, Simon & Schuster.

_____. (1996). *Quicker Than the Eye.* London, Simon & Schuster.

_____. (1988). *The Toynbee Convector.* London, Bantam.

Colwell, Stella. (2003). *Tracing Your Family History.* London: Faber and Faber.

Crowther, Bosley. (1987). *Laurel and Hardy: Clown Princes of Comedy.* London: Columbus.

Curran, Ron. (2009). *North Shields. The Bombing of a Town.* Newcastle: Summerhill Books.

Everson, William K. (1967). *The Films of Laurel and Hardy.* Secaucus, NJ: The Citadel Press.

Gehring, W.D. (1990). *Laurel & Hardy: A Bio-Bibliography.* New York: Greenwood Press.

Giusti, M. (1978). *Laurel & Hardy.* Firenze: La nuova Italia.

Grant, N. (1994). *Laurel & Hardy.* Bristol: Parragon.

Guiles, Fred Lawrence. (1995). *Stan: The Life of Stan Laurel.* London: Michael Joseph.

Harmon, L. (1973). *Larry Harmon's Laurel & Hardy.* London: Williams.

Harness, K., J. Larrabee and J.V. Brennan. (2006). *The Art of Laurel and Hardy: Graceful Calamity in the Films.* Jefferson NC: McFarland.

Hoppe, H. (2001). *Laurel & Hardy: Life & Magic.* Berlin: Trescher Verlag; Lancaster: Gazelle.

Jefferson, A. (1939). *Turning the Pages.* Unpublished manuscript.

Kaye, M. (1979). *The Laurel & Hardy Murders.* South Yarmouth, MA: J. Curley.

King, Robert. (1948). *North Shields Theatres.* Gateshead: Northumberland Press.

Lacourbe, R. (1975). *Laurel et Hardy; ou, L'enfance de l'art.* Paris: Seghers.

Louvish, S. (2002). *Stan and Ollie: The Roots of Comedy: The Double Life of Laurel and Hardy.* London: Faber.

Bibliography

MacGillivray, Scott (1998). *Laurel & Hardy: From the Forties Forward*. Lanham, MD: Vestal Press.

Marriot, A. J. (1993). *Laurel & Hardy: The British Tours*. Blackpool: A.J. Marriot.

McCabe, John. (2004). *Comedy World of Stan Laurel*. [S.l.], Doubleday.

_____. (1976). *Mr. Laurel and Mr. Hardy*. London: Robson Books.

McFerren, Robert & Tracy. (1997). *Laurel and Hardy in "Big Quizness."* Salem, OH: Plum Tree.

McGarry, A. (1992). *Laurel & Hardy*. Secaucus, NJ: Chartwell Books.

McGrath, T. (2005). *Laurel and Hardy*. Edinburgh: Capercaillie Books.

McIntyre, W. (1998). *The Laurel & Hardy Digest: A Cocktail of Lore, Love and Hisses*. Largs: W. McIntyre.

Mitchell, G. (1995). *The Laurel & Hardy Encyclopaedia*. London: Batsford.

Nollen, S.A. (1989). *The Boys: The Cinematic World of Laurel and Hardy*. Jefferson, NC: McFarland.

Owen-Pawson, J., and B. Mouland. (1984). *Laurel Before Hardy*. Kendal: Westmorland Gazette.

Owst, K. (1990). *Laurel and Hardy in Hull*. Beverley: Highgate.

Robb, B.J. (2001). *The Pocket Essential Laurel & Hardy*. Harpenden: Pocket Essentials.

Sanders, J. (1995). *Another Fine Dress: Role-Play in the Films of Laurel and Hardy*. London: Cassell.

Scagnetti, J. (1976). *The Laurel and Hardy Scrapbook*. Middle Village, NY: Jonathan David.

Shotton, Jack. (2010). *North Shields: Stepping Back in Time*. Newcastle: Summerhill Books.

Skretvedt, R. (1988). *Laurel and Hardy: The Magic Behind the Movies*. London: Apollo.

Thinès, G. (1998). *Laurel et Hardy; ou, Les Miroirs Deformants*. Bruxelles: La Lettre voleè.

Websites

Ancestry.com, the genealogical website: http://content.ancestry.co.uk/iexec/?htx=List&dbid=1025&offerid=0%3a7858%3a0

Another Fine Mess (Northern Ireland Laurel and Hardy Appreciation Society): http://www.anotherfinesite.com

Arnold, Gary: Stan Laurel Letters: http://www.stanlaurelletters.com/

Bacongrabbers (North-West UK Laurel and Hardy Appreciation Society): www.neilevans.pwp.blueyonder.co.uk

The Crazy World of Laurel and Hardy: http://www.stanlaurelandoliverhardy.com

Haurel and Lardy (Laurel and Hardy look-alikes): www.haurelandlardy.com

The International Laurel and Hardy Appreciation Society: www.sotd.org

Jefferson/Gough family history website: http://freepages.genealogy.rootsweb.ancestry.com/~andrewgough/ACFGough.htm; andrewgoughuk@yahoo.co.uk

Laurel and Hardie (look-alikes): www.laurelandhardylookalikes.com

Laurel and Hardy. The British Tours: www.laurelandhardythebritishtours.com; ajmarriot@aol.com

Laurel and Hardy. The Official Website.: www.laurel-and-hardy.com

Laurel and Hardy Central: www.laurelandhardycentral.com

Laurel and Hardy Films: http://laurelandhardyfilms.com/#/

Bibliography

The Laurel and Hardy Forum: http://www.laurelandhardyforum.com

The Laurel and Hardy Informant: www.blotto-online.com

The Laurel and Hardy Magazine: http://www.laurelandhardy.org

Laurel and Hardy Museum (Germany): www.laurel-hardy-museum.de

The Laurel and Hardy Museum (Harlem, Georgia): http://laurelandhardymuseum.org

Laurel and Hardy Museum (Ulverston, UK): www.laurel-and-hardy.co.uk

Laurel and Hardy Society Way Out West Tent (Los Angeles): www.wayoutwest.org

The Laurel and Hardy Story (Italy): http://www.laurel-e-hardy.it

Letters from Stan. The Stan Laurel Correspondence Archive Project: http://letters
fromstan.com; info@lettersfromstan.com

Nutty News Network: http://www.nuttynutnewsnetwork.com/

Shovlin, Texas Pete: http://lettersfromstan.com/stan_texaspete.html; http://www.
myspace.com/texaspeteshovlin/music/songs/letter-from-stan-4881005

YouTube: Stanlio and Ollio — Laurel and Hardy in Tynemouth followed by Stan Laurel
with his father A.J. in London (1932): http://www.youtube.com/watch?v=9by8l5
GrVCM

Index

Index

196

Index

Index

Index